A Passion for Quilting

35 step-by-step patchwork and quilting projects

Nicki Trench

CICO BOOKS

LONDON NEW YORK

This edition published in 2018 by CICO Books
An imprint of Ryland Peters & Small Ltd
20–21 Jockey's Fields, London WC1R 4BW
341 E 116th Street, New York, NY 10029

www.rylandpeters.com

10 9 8 7 6 5 4 3 2 1

First published in 2012
Text © Nicki Trench 2012
Design and photography © CICO Books 2012

A CIP catalog record for this book is
available from the Library of Congress
and the British Library.

ISBN: 978 1 78249 584 0

Printed in China

Editor: Sarah Hoggett
Designer: Mark Latter
Photographers: Emma Mitchell & Holly Jolliffe
Stylists: Rose Hammick & Tanya Goodwin
Cut-out photographer: Martin Norris
Step illustrators: Kate Simunek & Michael Hill
Template illustrator: Stephen Dew

contents

introduction

If you have a passion for fabrics, this is the book for you. Whether you're a complete beginner or an experienced quilter, the designs all have a contemporary twist and use a mix of modern, retro and vintage fabrics that you're going to love: there really is something for everyone.

When it comes to quilting or patchwork, I defy convention whenever possible. Many people are freaked out by quilting books because they tend to be full of complicated quilting jargon and mathematical drawings—and although I have a great love of sewing and fabrics, this lack of accessibility is something that has, in the past, driven me to the cookery section of a book store (something more in my comfort zone). If anyone tells you that you can't do quilting, don't take any notice. I've often been told that I couldn't do this or that and been met with gasps of, "But you're supposed to...". Forget that. Quilts were never supposed to be perfect and they really don't have to be difficult: they are works of art and who cares if there is an irregularity or two—it's all part of the charm.

In this book we have worked to make the projects simple, easy to understand, and pretty at the same time. inspiration lies in the gorgeous fabrics, which are getting more and more exciting to buy. Fabric stores are undergoing a resurgence and have introduced a range of modern and vintage-style prints. There are retro feedsacks, a take on some interesting 1920s and 1930s designs, florals, stripes, dots, and geometrics. In this book I've also cut up a collection of vintage embroideries, dish towels, and tablecloths to make bunting, quilts, and accessories.

I have had so much fun trailing around vintage shops, internet fabric sites, fabric stores, and my mother's and friends' old cupboards. Once you get into quilting, you'll start looking at old clothing in a different way. When my children were small I could never throw away their dresses or school uniforms as there were so many happy memories attached to them; instead, I eventually turned their dress scraps into quilts for their 18th and 21st birthdays (see Camilla's Quilt, page 14). It's comforting to know that in their drafty shared university houses, they are tucked up beneath all the fabrics from their childhood, turned lovingly into something warm and aesthetically pleasing.

Of course, there have to be some basic safety guidelines you must follow. You will be using some sharp and potentially dangerous implements. Take care not to stab through your fingers with the sewing machine needle; use scissors, rotary cutters, seam rippers, pins, and irons with great care.

Use a decent thread! I use an Italian brand called Aurifil. Their color palette suits the range of fabrics that I've chosen and they are excellent quality. It's worth investing in a good brand. I've taken short cuts in the past and bought cheap threads from eBay, only to find that they snap easily and mangle up my machine when I'm right in the middle of sewing a large quilt.

It's important to consider your equipment carefully. You don't have to spend a fortune on quilting or patchwork, but it's worth investing in a decent sewing machine,

rotary cutter, cutting board, good sharp scissors, and a tape measure. Many machines come with a variety of feet; if you can, buy a walking foot, which holds the quilt sandwich in place and makes life a lot easier—but don't be put off if you haven't got one. There are all sorts of quilting gadgets out there. Don't worry about those—you can buy them later if you want to—but just get started, even if you own only a pair of scissors.

Go ahead, dive in, and enjoy the ride—it'll be a long and hugely satisfying one and you'll never touch a cookery book again: you'll be too busy quilting!

blankets & quilts

log cabin quilt

This is one of my favorite quilts ever. I haven't used the traditional Log Cabin method, where one side is in light shades and the other dark: instead, I've just chosen fabrics that I love and put them together. I tried to choose dominant colors of reds, yellows, greens, and blues with a white background to make the quilt look crisp and modern. This quilt is made up of 30 bright blocks. Each block measures approx. 12 in. (30 cm) when the quilt is completed.

YOU WILL NEED

4 yd (4 m) of an assortment of brightly colored spotted, striped, floral, and geometric cotton print fabrics for the patchwork

2 yd (2 m) red-and-white floral cotton fabric, 60 in. (152 cm) wide, for backing

74 x 62 in. (188 x 158 cm) batting (wadding)

¾ yd (75 cm) plain red cotton fabric, 2½ in. (6 cm) wide, for binding

finished size:

Approx. 72 x 60 in. (183 x 152 cm)

1 Press the fabrics for the patchwork. Cut strips of fabric 2 in. (5 cm) wide. These will be added from the center outward to make the block, so will range in length from 2 in. (5 cm) at the center to 12½ in. (32 cm) at the outer edges. Decide—roughly—on the arrangement of the strips in the block.

2 Take one of the fabrics that will be at the center of the block and cut across it at right angles to a length of 2 in. (5 cm), giving a 2-in. (5-cm) square. Cut the second center square in a different fabric in the same way.

3 Pin the two squares right sides together and, using a ¼-in. (6-mm) foot on the machine, join them on one side with a ¼-in. (6-mm) seam. Press the seam open.

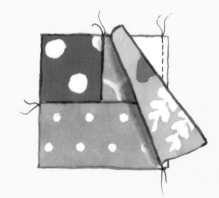

4 Pin another length of fabric right sides together along one long edge of the pressed unit and attach it in the same way. Trim the edge level with the first pressed unit after sewing. Press the seam open.

5 Attach another strip across the two pieces just joined. Again, trim the edge level after sewing and press the seam open.

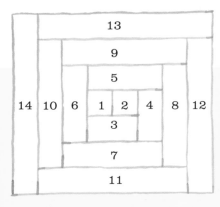

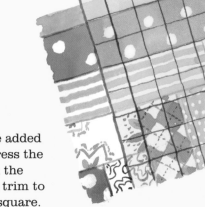

6 Keep adding strips in the order shown in the diagram. Remember to press the seam open each time you add a strip, and measure the total width of the piece periodically to ensure that the seams are accurate.

7 When you have added the final strip, press the block, place it on the cutting mat, and trim to 12½ in. (32 cm) square.

8 Repeat steps 1–5 to make 30 log cabin blocks in the same way. Arrange the blocks in six rows of five blocks each. Sew the blocks together in horizontal rows, pressing the seams open each time, then sew the rows together to complete the quilt top. Press the quilt top well on the right side of the fabric.

9 Assemble the three layers of the quilt "sandwich" (see page 133). Using curved safety pins and starting in the center of the quilt and working outward, pin through all layers to secure well, smoothing the quilt as you go.

10 Using a walking foot on your machine, if you have one, and a light-colored thread, start at one corner of the quilt and sew a meandering (curving) line with wide twists diagonally across the quilt. The stitching should pass through the corner of each block. When the first diagonal row is completed, repeat for each diagonal row in one direction.

11 Starting from the opposite corner, repeat the process, making sure the quilt is smooth and unpuckered when one line of quilt stitching crosses another. This is best done by smoothing with both hands while sewing and is important on a large quilt. Trim the backing fabric and batting (wadding) level with the quilt top if necessary.

12 Cut strips of binding fabric on the straight grain, 2½ in. (6.5 cm) wide. You will need two strips measuring the same as the top of the quilt, and two measuring the same as the sides plus 1 in. (2.5 cm). Bind the quilt, using one of the methods on pages 136–137.

Camilla's quilt

This is a quilt that I made for my daughter's 21st birthday. She chose the fabrics from scraps in my cupboard and added a few more from her old dresses and curtains from her bedroom as a child.

level: beginner

YOU WILL NEED

154 x 6½-in. (17-cm) squares in cotton fabrics of your choice

88½ x 71 in. (228 x 180 cm) cotton fabric for backing

88½ x 71 in. (228 x 180 cm) batting (wadding)

finished size:

84½ x 66½ in. (222.5 x 175 cm)

1 Using a homemade template or a rotary cutter and quilter's rule on a cutting mat (see page 128), cut out 154 6½-in. (17-cm) squares in fabrics of your choice. Lay them out on a flat surface and arrange them in 14 rows of 11 squares each. Label the rows and the order of the squares (see page 130).

2 Right sides together, using ¼-in. (6-mm) seams and making sure you keep the squares in order, machine stitch the squares in each row together. Press the seams in each row to one side, all in the same direction.

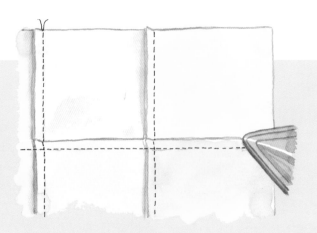

3 Machine stitch the rows together, again using ¼-in. (6-mm) seams. Press the seams to one side, all in the same direction. Turn the quilt top over and press all the seams on the right side.

4 Cut a piece of backing fabric 2 in. (5 cm) larger all around than the quilt top, as this quilt is self-bound (see page 136). If your fabric isn't wide enough, cut two lengths and join them together in the center.

5 Assemble the quilt "sandwich" (see page 133), centering the batting (wadding) and quilt top on the backing fabric.

6 Starting from the center line, quilt "in the ditch" (see page 134) across the quilt from one side to the other. Turn the quilt through 90 degrees and quilt through the center again from top to bottom, making sure the quilt is smooth and unpuckered where one line of quilting crosses another. Continue in this way, quilting along each seam of the patchwork.

7 Trim the batting (wadding) to the same size as the quilt top, if necessary; do not trim the backing fabric.

8 Bind the quilt, following the instructions for Self Binding on page 136.

buggy blanket

This cute buggy blanket is just the right size for a buggy or car seat. Freehand embroidery is a wonderful way to appliqué. The edges may fray, but this will give your work an interesting textured look. Use a fabric adhesive spray to hold the shapes in place while

level: experienced

YOU WILL NEED

Piece 1: 23 x 13½ in. (58.5 x 34.5 cm) pale green/blue fabric

Piece 2: 23 x 2½ in. (58.5 x 6 cm) pink spotted fabric

Piece 3: 23 x 16¾ in. (58.5 x 42.5 cm) bright green/blue fabric

29 x 23 in. (73.5 x 58.5 cm) cotton fabric for backing

29 x 23 in. (73.5 x 58.5 cm) batting (wadding)

Templates on page 139

Scraps of fabric for the appliqué motifs: brown and yellow (bees); pink and green spotted (bees' wings); yellow, pink, orange, and red florals (bunting flags and flowers)

Approx. 45 in. (114 cm) yellow ribbon, ¼ in. (6 mm) wide, for the flower stalks

Approx. 26 in. (66 cm) ribbon, ¼ in. (6 mm) wide, for the bunting ribbon

Approx 114 in. (290 cm) green spotted fabric, 2½ in. (6 cm) wide, for binding

Colored threads for freehand embroidery

Fabric adhesive spray

finished size:
29 x 23 in. (76.5 x 58.5 cm)

1 Taking a ⅝-in. (1.5-cm) seam, machine stitch pieces 1, 2, and 3 together along their long edges. Press open the seams. Turn the piece over and press again on the right side.

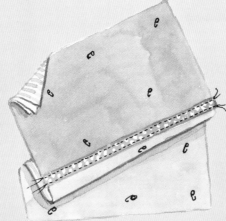
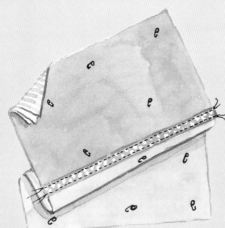

2 Place the backing fabric right side down on a flat surface, with the batting (wadding) on top, and the blanket top right side up on top of the batting. Working from the center outward, using curved safety pins, pin the three layers together.

3 Machine embroider freehand along the middle strip of fabric, using a contrasting color of thread.

4 Enlarge the bunting flags, bee, and flower templates on page 139 by 200 percent and cut out. Pin the paper templates to the appropriate fabrics and cut out. Arrange the motifs on the blanket.

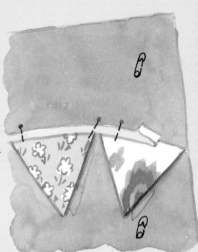

5 Place the bunting ribbon over the top edges of the bunting flags and pin it in place. Using a contrasting color of thread, machine stitch the ribbon in place.

6 Machine stitch two or three lines of stitching around the bunting flags; you can use just one color of thread or several for contrast.

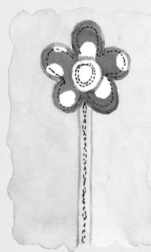

7 Sew on the other motifs in the same way, experimenting with different colors of thread to create different effects. For the flower motifs make sure you sew on thin ribbon for the stalks before adding the flower heads.

8 Quilt some stitches to show the bees flying. If you're not confident about doing this freehand, mark out the quilting line with tailor's chalk.

9 Cut strips of binding fabric on the straight grain, 2⅛ in. (6.5 cm) wide. You will need two strips measuring the same as the top of the quilt, and two measuring the same as the sides plus 1 in. (2.5 cm). Bind the blanket, using one of the methods on pages 136–137.

retro crib quilt

This vintage-style quilt is made with retro print fabrics and backed with a supersoft fleece; it needs no batting (wadding).

YOU WILL NEED

54 x 4¼-in. (11-cm) squares in a variety of retro print cotton fabrics

54 x 4¼-in. (11-cm) squares in light brown/white checked fabric

39 x 59 in. (1 x 1.5 m) supersoft fleece, off white, for the backing

Two 37½ x 1-in. (95 x 2.5 cm) and two 49 x 1-in. (1.25 m x 2.5 cm) strips of cotton fabric for the binding

173 in. (440 cm) yellow bobble trim

finished size:

35½ x 47 in. (90 x 121 cm)

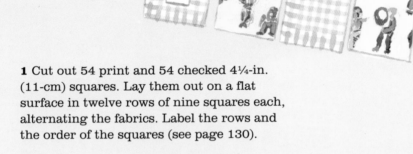

1 Cut out 54 print and 54 checked 4¼-in. (11-cm) squares. Lay them out on a flat surface in twelve rows of nine squares each, alternating the fabrics. Label the rows and the order of the squares (see page 130).

2 Right sides together, taking ¼-in. (6-mm) seams and making sure you keep the squares in order, machine stitch the squares in each row together. Press the seams in each row to one side, all in the same direction.

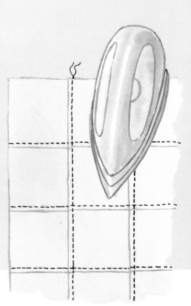

3 Machine stitch the rows together, again taking ¼-in. (6-mm) seams. Press the seams to one side, all in the same direction.

4 Turn the quilt top right side up and press well.

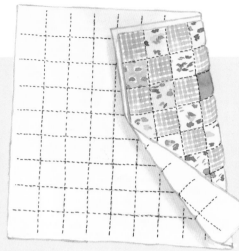

5 Cut the fleece fabric 2 in. (5 cm) larger all around than the patchwork and place it right side down on a flat surface. Center the patchwork right side up on top and smooth out the fabric. Working from the center outward, using curved safety pins, pin the layers together.

6 Starting from the center line, quilt "in the ditch" (see page 134) across the quilt from side to side. Turn the quilt though 90 degrees and quilt through the center seam again, forming a cross. Make sure the quilt is smooth and unpuckered where one line of quilting crosses another. Trim all edges level.

7 Lay the quilt out on a flat surface and lightly mark the center of each checked square. Thread a needle with yarn and insert it into the patchwork top (not the backing) about ⅛ in. (2–3 mm) above the center point. Bring the needle up on the top of the quilt, ⅛ in. (2–3 mm) below the center point, leaving a long tail on each side of the center point. Cut the yarn.

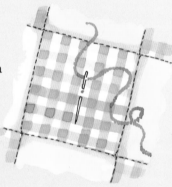

9 Pick up four strands in each hand and tie together in a double knot. Repeat steps 7–9 in all checked squares.

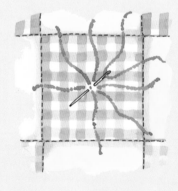

8 Repeat to the left and right of the center point so there's one strand at each "compass point", and then in between the "compass points", so that you have eight strands. Pick up two adjacent strands on one side and two on the opposite side and tie in a single knot. Turn the quilt through 90° and repeat the tying process.

10 Cut strips of binding fabric on the straight grain, 2⅛ in. (6.5 cm) wide. You will need two strips measuring the same as the top of the quilt, and two measuring the same as the sides plus 1 in. (2.5 cm). Bind the quilt, using one of the methods on pages 136–137.

11 Pin, then machine or hand stitch bobble trim around the right side edges of the quilt.

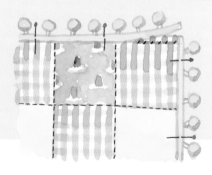

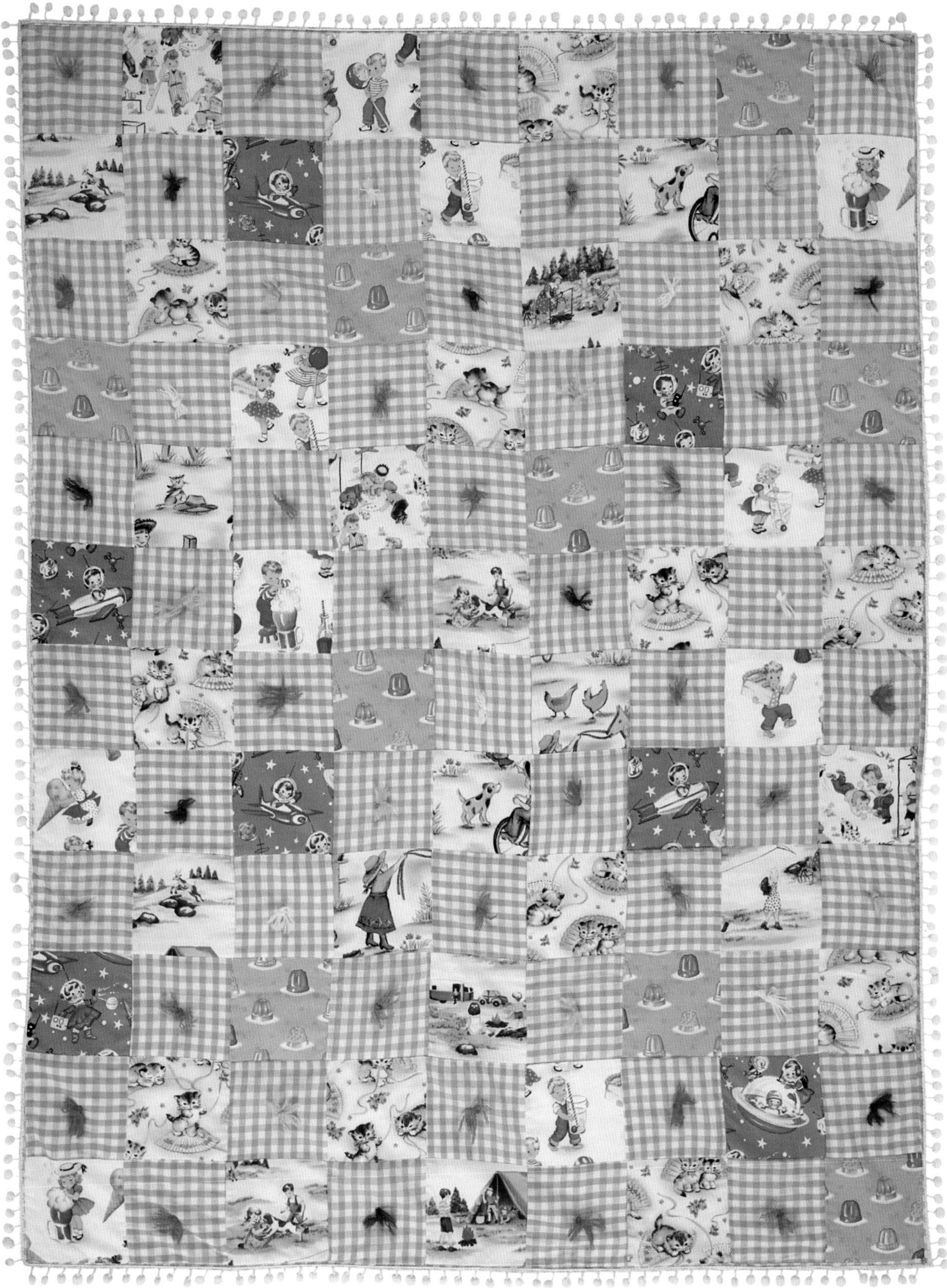

Ohio star quilt

This quilt shows a traditional Ohio Star pattern, where the stars contrast dark and light alternately, but try experimenting and use your own color combinations.

YOU WILL NEED

1 yd (1 m) dark cream cotton fabric

1 yd (1 m) beige cotton fabric

1 yd (1 m) red spotted cotton fabric

1 yd (1 m) pale blue cotton fabric

1 yd (1 m) floral print cotton fabric

1 yd (1 m) light cream cotton fabric

50 x 62 in. (127 x 157.5 cm) red spotted fabric for backing

50 x 62 in. (127 x 157.5 cm) batting (wadding)

finished size:

46 x 58 in. (117 x 147 cm)

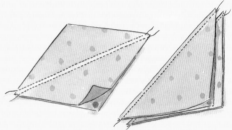

1 To make the dark blocks, draw a diagonal line across the back of the two 3-in. (7.5-cm) red spotted squares. With right sides together, place one red square on top of a 3-in. (7.5-cm) pale blue square. Machine stitch down both sides of the diagonal line, ¼ in. (6 mm) from the line. Cut along the drawn center line.

2 Open out each half square triangle and press the seam toward the darker fabric. Trim the "ears."

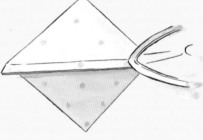

cutting the star blocks

For each dark star block, cut:
1 x 2-in. (5-cm) red spotted square
4 x 2-in. (5-cm) pale blue squares
2 x 3-in. (7.5-cm) pale blue squares
2 x 3-in. (7.5-cm) red spotted squares

For each light star block, cut:
1 x 2-in. (5-cm) floral square
4 x 2-in. (5-cm) light cream squares
2 x 3-in. (7.5-cm) light cream squares
2 x 3-in. (7.5-cm) floral squares

Make 32 dark star blocks and 31 light star blocks. Each finished block measures 4½ in. (11.5 cm).

3 Mark another diagonal line across the seamline of the two red/blue squares and cut along the line. You now have eight two-color triangles.

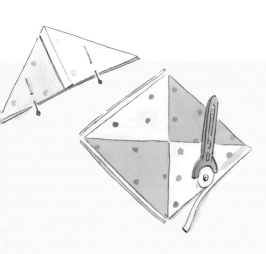

4 With rights sides together, pair up triangles with colors opposite each other. Using a ¼-in. (6-mm) seam, pin and sew along the long edge to make a square. Open out the seam and press. Trim the squares to 2 in. (5 cm), making sure the diagonal seams run across the center.

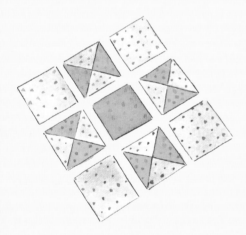

5 To complete the dark star block, lay out the units as shown, with a red spotted square in the center and pale blue squares in the corners. Machine stitch the horizontal rows together first, using a ¼-in. (6-mm) seam, then press the seams to one side, all in the same direction. Then sew the rows together, again using a ¼-in. (6-mm) seam, and press the seams to one side, all in the same direction.

6 Repeat steps 1–5 to make 32 dark star blocks. Then make 31 light star blocks, replacing the red spotted fabric with a floral print and the pale blue with a light cream fabric.

7 For the solid (plain) blocks, cut 32 5-in. (13-cm) beige squares and 32 5-in. (13-cm) dark cream squares. Cut eight of each color of square in half diagonally, then cut one beige and one dark cream triangle in half.

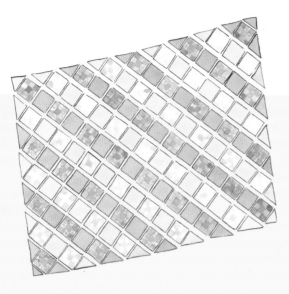

8 On a flat surface, lay out the blocks as shown, with two dark cream corners opposite each other and two beige corners in the other corners. With right sides together, pin the seams of the square blocks in diagonal strips. Machine stitch together, using a ¼-in. (6-mm) seam. Press the seams to one side.

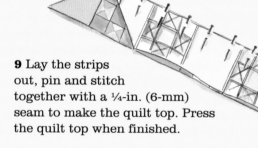

9 Lay the strips out, pin and stitch together with a ¼-in. (6-mm) seam to make the quilt top. Press the quilt top when finished.

10 Cut a piece of backing fabric 2 in. (5 cm) larger all around than the quilt top, as this quilt is self-bound (see page 136). If your fabric isn't wide enough, cut two lengths and join them together in the center.

11 Assemble the quilt "sandwich" (see page 133), centering the batting (wadding) and quilt top on the backing fabric.

12 Quilt "in the ditch" (see page 134) around the outside of each plain and patterned square, then quilt diagonal lines (see page 135) from cover to cover in both directions for each large plain and patterned square. Make sure the quilt is smooth and unpuckered where one line of quilting crosses another.

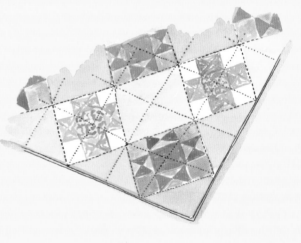

13 Trim the batting (wadding) to the same size as the quilt top; do not trim the backing fabric. Bind the quilt, following the instructions for Self Binding on page 136.

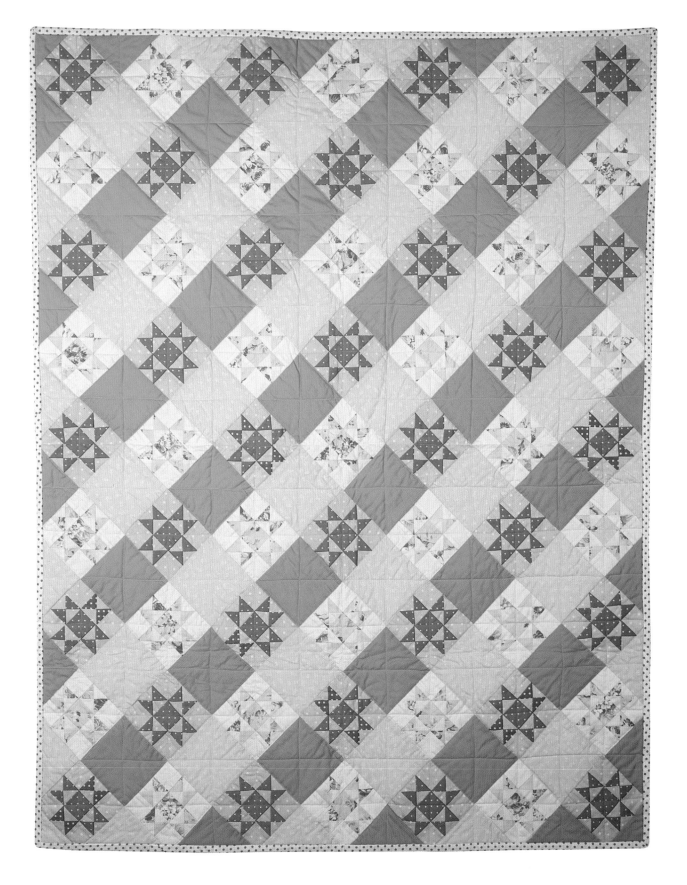

vintage embroidered quilt

Many of the blocks in this quilt were made using vintage traycloths that are exactly the right size. Alternatively, look out for old and damaged tablecloths that can be cut to size. Don't feel guilty about cutting them up: you're going to revitalize them and give them a new lease on life.

---

level: beginner

YOU WILL NEED

35 13 x 18-in. (33 x 46-cm) blocks of vintage embroidery

111 x 85 in. (282 x 216 cm) toile de jouy fabric for backing

111 x 85 in. (282 x 216 cm) batting (wadding)

Two 103 x 4½-in. (262 x 11.5-cm) and two 77 x 4½-in. (196 x 11.5-cm) strips of white cotton fabric for borders

10 yd (9.15 m) navy blue rick-rack

10¼ yd (9.4 m) embroidered ribbon, 1 in. (2.5 cm) wide

finished size:

95 x 84 in. (242 x 213 cm)

1 Lay the embroidered blocks out on a flat surface and arrange them in six rows of five. Label the rows and the order of the blocks (see page 130).

2 Right sides together, using ¼-in. (6-mm) seams and making sure you keep the blocks in order, machine stitch the blocks in each row together. Press the seams in each row to one side, all in the same direction. Machine stitch the rows together, again using ¼-in. (6-mm) seams. Press the seams to one side, all in the same direction. Turn the quilt top over and press the whole quilt on the right side.

3 Cut two 77 x 4½-in. (196 x 11.5-cm) and two 103 x 4½-in. (262 x 11.5-cm) strips of white cotton fabric for the borders. With right sides together, using ¼-in. (6-mm) seams, pin and machine stitch the short strips to the top and bottom of the quilt. Press the seams to one side and trim the side edges level with the quilt top. Pin and machine stitch the long strips to the side edges of the quilt. Press the seams to one side and trim the edges. Press the quilt on the right side.

re-using vintage embroideries

When cutting out blocks of vintage embroideries, make sure you trim off thick edges and old hems from old traycloths. If cutting out from tablecloths, "fussy pick" (see page 128) your designs so that you only cut out and use the best bits. Many old tray and tablecloths have stains on them, so make sure you avoid those areas.

4 Measure out 1 in. (2.5 cm) from the seam between the pieced quilt top and the border all around, pin rick-rack in place, and machine stitch.

5 Cut the backing fabric and batting (wadding) to the size of the quilt top plus 2 in. (5 cm) all around. Assemble the quilt "sandwich" (see page 133), centering the batting (wadding) and quilt top on the backing fabric. Using curved safety pins and starting in the center of the quilt and working outward, pin through all layers to secure well, smoothing the fabric as you go.

cutting the backing fabric

If your fabric isn't wide enough, cut two lengths, join them together, and press the seam open.

6 Using a walking foot if possible, starting with the center seams and working outward, quilt "in the ditch" (see page 134) along each seam line.

7 Lay the quilt out flat again. Smooth out the border and pin it to the batting (wadding) and backing to hold it in position. Lift up the edge of the border and mark the batting (wadding) ½ in. (1 cm) in from the edge of the quilt top. Trim the batting (wadding) along the marked line.

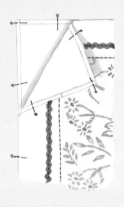

8 Trim the backing fabric to the same size as the quilt top. Turn the quilt top edges over the batting (wadding) and pin, so that the top edges cover the batting (wadding). Fold the backing fabric to the inside to align with the quilt top and pin together, so that both edges are turned in toward each other. Press all edges.

9 Pin the border ribbon around all edges, folding it under at the corners for a neat finish. Machine stitch the ribbon onto the quilt.

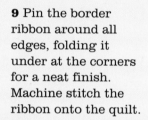

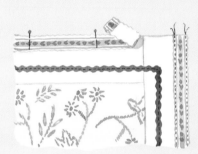

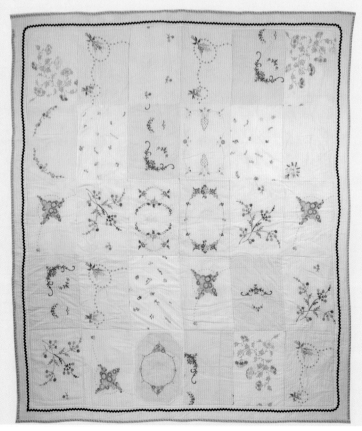

10 Using a neutral thread and a darning/embroidery foot on your machine, lower the feed dogs and machine stitch one flower in the center of each block. If you prefer, you can mark the flower on the fabric using a fade-away fabric marker pen.

quilted flowers

Practice these flowers first on a mini quilt sandwich. You may need to set a smaller stitch size and adjust the tension on your machine until they look right.

rose cottage quilt

This is a very joyful quilt that uses bright and cheerful floral squares with toile de jouy rectangles and a spotty backing.

YOU WILL NEED

1 yd (1 m) floral fabric

5 ft (1.5 m) toile de jouy fabric

50 x 59 in. (127 x 150 cm) wadding (batting)

50 x 59 in. (127 x 150 cm) backing fabric

finished size:

48 x 57 in. (122 x 145 cm)

1 Cut 30 6½-in. (16.5-cm) squares of floral fabric and 24 6½ x 3½-in. (16.5 x 9-cm) rectangles of toile de jouy.

2 With right sides together, using a ¼-in. (6-mm) seam, pin and stitch one rectangle to one square. Press the seams to one side. Repeat to make 24 rectangle/square pairs.

3 Sew four pairs in strips horizontally, adding one extra floral square on the end. Repeat five times, so that you have six strips.

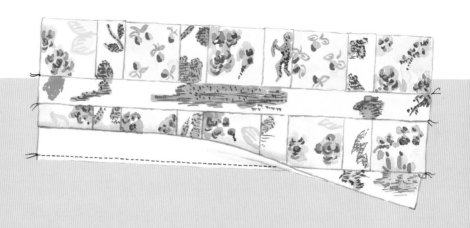

4 Cut five 42½ x 3½ (108 x 9-cm) strips of toile de jouy fabric. With right sides together, using a ¼-in. (6-mm) seam, pin and machine stitch one toile de jouy strip between each strip of rectangles and squares. Press the seams to one side.

5 Cut two 51½ x 3½-in. (131 x 9-cm) and two 48½ x 3½-in. (123 x 9-cm) strips of toile de jouy fabric for the borders. With right sides together, using a ¼-in. (6-mm) seam, pin and machine stitch one long strip to each side of the quilt and press the seams to one side. Then stitch the short strips to the top and bottom of the quilt and press the seams to one side. Trim the edges straight if necessary. Press the quilt top well from the right side.

6 Cut a piece of backing fabric 2 in. (5 cm) larger all around than the quilt top, as this quilt is self-bound (see page 136). If your fabric isn't wide enough, cut two lengths and join them together.

7 Assemble the quilt "sandwich" (see page 133), centering the batting (wadding) and quilt top on the backing fabric.

8 Meander quilt along the toile de jouy borders and across the whole quilt, and quilt "in the ditch" along each seam of each square (see pages 134–5).

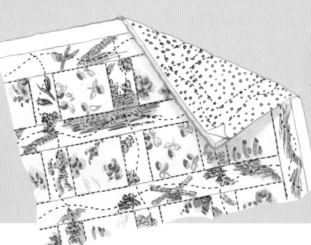

9 Trim the batting (wadding) to the same size as the quilt top, if necessary; do not trim the backing fabric.

10 Bind the quilt, following the instructions for Self Binding on page 136.

Besh's crib quilt

This is a very simple and easy quilt for a baby's crib, alternating small patterned squares with appliquéd squares. You can download free appliqué shapes from the Internet; alternatively, draw your own shapes. Spray fabric adhesive onto the back of the appliqué shapes to hold them in position while you sew them in place.

level: beginner

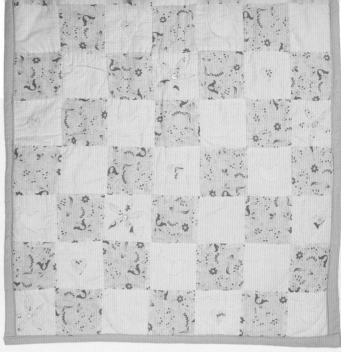

YOU WILL NEED

Assorted fabric scraps for appliqué

32 x 4½-in. (11.5-cm) squares of solid (plain) fabric

31 x 4½-in. (11.5-cm) squares of patterned fabric

30½ x 38½ in. (82.5 x 104.5 cm) fleece for backing

Two 29½ x 2½-in. (80 x 6-cm) and two 37½ x 2½-in. (102 x 6-cm) strips of cotton fabric for binding

finished size:

28½ x 36½ in. (77.5 x 99.5 cm)

1 Appliqué your chosen designs onto the solid (plain) squares (see page 132). On a flat surface, alternating patterned and appliquéd squares, arrange the squares in nine rows of seven squares each. Label the rows and the order of the squares (see page 130).

2 Right sides together, using ¼-in. (6-mm) seams and making sure you keep the squares in order, machine stitch the squares in each row together. Press the seams in each row to one side, all in the same direction.

3 Machine stitch the rows together, again using ¼-in. (6-mm) seams. Press the seams to one side, all in the same direction. Turn the quilt top over and press on the right side.

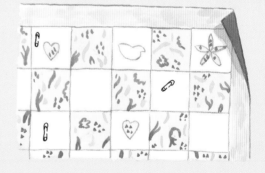

4 Cut the fleece fabric 2 in. (5 cm) larger all around than the patchwork and place it right side down on a flat surface. Center the patchwork right side up on top and smooth out the fabric. Working from the center outward, using curved safety pins, pin the layers together.

5 Starting from the center line, quilt "in the ditch" (see page 134) across the quilt from side to side. Turn the quilt though 90 degrees and quilt through the center seam again, forming a cross. Make sure the quilt is smooth and unpuckered where one line of quilting crosses another. Trim the fleece level with the quilt top.

6 Cut strips of binding fabric on the straight grain, 2½ in. (6.5 cm) wide. You will need two strips measuring the same as the top of the quilt plus 1 in. (2.5 cm), and two measuring the same as the sides plus 1 in. (2.5 cm). Bind the quilt, using one of the methods on pages 136–7.

baby star mat

A traditional diamond star pattern using some retro prints and bright spots combined together, this makes a lovely mat that you can fold up and take anywhere for baby to sit and play on.

1 Enlarge the template on page 139 by 200 percent and cut out. Using the template, cut three diamonds of spotted fabric and one of each patterned fabric for the star.

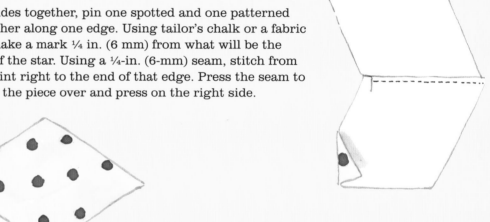

YOU WILL NEED

Template on page 139

22 x 20 in. (56 x 50 cm) spotted fabric for the star

22 x 20 in. (56 x 50 cm) patterned fabric in each of three designs for the star

Four x 2½-in. (6.5-cm) squares in each of four fabrics for the star corners

37 x 37 in. (94 x 94 cm) cream cotton fabric for the quilt top

37 x 37 in. (94 x 94 cm) red spotted fabric for backing

37 x 37 in. (94 x 94 cm) batting (wadding)

36 in. (91.5 cm) red rick-rack braid

Six x 4-in. (10-cm) lengths of ribbon, approx. ½ in. (15 mm) wide, in a variety of colors to match quilt

finished size:

34 x 34 in. (86.5 x 86.5 cm)

2 With right sides together, pin one spotted and one patterned diamond together along one edge. Using tailor's chalk or a fabric marker pen, make a mark ¼ in. (6 mm) from what will be the outside edge of the star. Using a ¼-in. (6-mm) seam, stitch from the marked point right to the end of that edge. Press the seam to one side. Turn the piece over and press on the right side.

3 Attach a different patterned diamond to the other edge of the spotted diamond in the same way to make up one half of the star.

4 Repeat steps 2 and 3 to make up the second half of the star—but this time, have a patterned piece in the center and a spotted piece on either side.

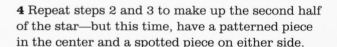

5 With right sides together, pin the two halves of the star together. Make a mark ¼ in. (6 mm) in from each end. Starting and ending at the marked points, using a ¼-in. (6-mm) seam, machine stitch the two halves together to form a 6-pointed star. Press the seam to one side. Turn the star over and press it on the right side. Turn the star over again, turn the raw edges under by ¼ in. (6 mm), and press. Fold the points under to make a neat edge.

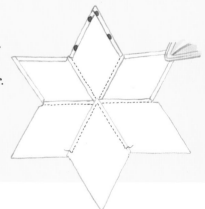

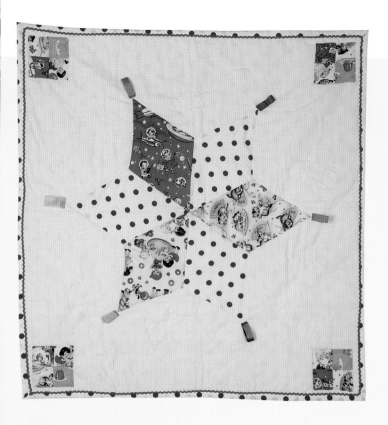

6 Mark the center point on the right side of the quilt top. Line up the center of the star with the center of the quilt top fabric. Starting at the center, pin the star to the quilt top fabric, smoothing it out flat as you go.

7 Lay the quilt top right side up on top of the batting (wadding). Smooth the layers and pin well. Starting from the center of the star and sewing out toward the points, quilt "in the ditch" (see page 134) along the seams and around the edges of the star.

stitch advice

When you've assembled the star, it may not be completely smooth, so press it well, starting from the center.

8 Trim the quilt top and batting (wadding) to 34 in. (86.5 cm) square. Trim the backing fabric to 1 in. (2.5 cm) larger all around than the quilt top.

9 Fold the backing fabric over the raw edge of the quilt top, so that all the raw edges are enclosed (see page 136). Pin close to the folded edge.

10 Pin rick-rack braid all around the edge of the quilt, on top of the binding. Using red top thread and cream thread in the bobbin, machine stitch the rick-rack in place.

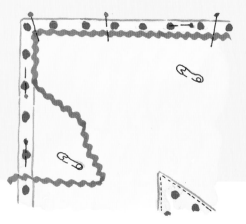

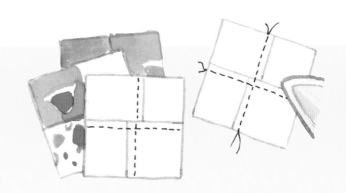

11 Arrange the corner squares in four groups of four. With right sides together, using a ¼-in. (6-mm) seam, machine stitch two squares of the first corner block together. Press the seam to one side. Turn the squares over to the right side and press again. Repeat with the remaining two squares, pressing the seam in the opposite direction. Then join the two rows of two squares together. Repeat, so that you have four four-square corner blocks.

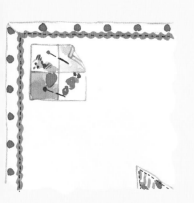

12 Fold each edge of each corner block under by ¼ in. (6 mm) and press. Pin one four-square block to each corner of the quilt, about ¼ in. (6 mm) from the edge. Quilt "in the ditch" (see page 134), along the seams of each square. Machine stitch around the edges, close to the edge.

13 Machine quilt motifs of your choice randomly around the outside of the star. Animals, teddy bears, flowers, and space ships all look great!

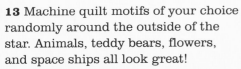

14 Fold six 4-in. (10-cm) lengths of ribbon in half widthwise. Fold the raw edges over and hand stitch to prevent fraying. Hand stitch a ribbon tab close to each point of the star.

bags & purses

stitch advice
When you've finished the patchwork, check whether any stitching between the hexagons has come loose and repair it if necessary.

California bag

YOU WILL NEED

Template on page 139

Paper for templates

26 x 26 in. (66 x 66 cm) fabric in total for patchwork

25 x 16½ in. (63.5 x 42 cm) lining fabric

79½ x 2½ in. (202 x 6 cm) binding

25 x 16½ in. (63.5 x 42 cm) batting (wadding)

Leather bag handles

finished size:
12½ x 13½ in. (32 x 34.5 cm)

This is a great portable project: the paper pieces and fabric scraps can be tucked into your handbag and brought out while you are waiting for a bus, picking the kids up from school, or watching TV. I've used five different fabrics, but this bag can be made using any combination, or even just one color.

1 Cut out the lining fabric, so that you can use it as a guide to check if you've made the right number of hexagon "flowers."

2 Cut out the template on page 139. You will need about 130 paper templates although, when all sides of a hexagon have been sewn to other hexagons, you can remove the basting (tacking) stitches and re-use the template.

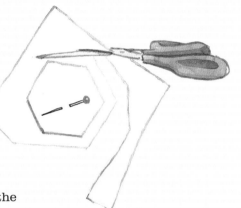

3 Place the template onto the fabric and cut around it, making sure you leave enough space around the hexagon to fold the fabric over to the wrong side.

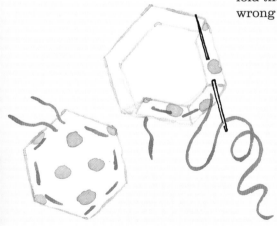

4 Center the paper hexagon on the fabric piece and fold the seam allowance along one side of the paper piece. Fingerpress to get a sharp crease, and baste (tack) in place. Repeat around each side of the hexagon, folding each corner in neatly and stitching through the fold to secure. Prepare about 130 hexagons in this way.

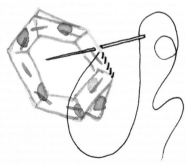

5 Each flower is made up of six hexagon "petals" and one central piece. Hold the center hexagon and one petal right sides together and whipstitch (see page 138) them together along one edge.

6 Add the remaining petals for each flower in the same way, whipstitching the edge adjoining the center first, and then the edge between that petal and the previous one. Make 36 flowers in different color combinations. Join the flowers together in approx. eight rows of four or five flowers each, to make a piece of patchwork fabric slightly larger than the lining piece.

7 Take out the basting (tacking) stitches and paper templates. Using a rotary cutter and quilter's rule on a cutting mat, trim the patchwork piece around the edges to the same size as the lining fabric. Press the patchwork from the right side.

8 Cut the batting (wadding) to size. All three pieces—patchwork, batting (wadding), and lining fabric—should be the same size.

9 On a flat surface place, place the patchwork right side down, with the batting (wadding) on top and the lining fabric right side up on top of the batting (wadding). Pin the layers together.

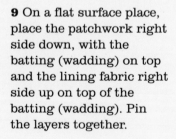

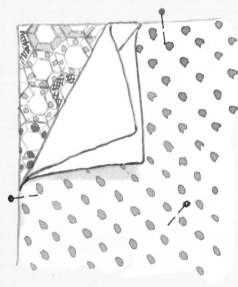

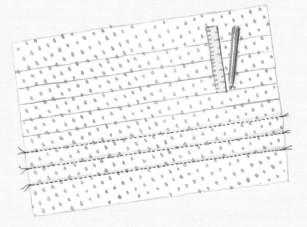

10 Starting 3 in. (7.5 cm) in from one side edge, mark out straight lines about 1½ in. (4 cm) apart with marker chalk or pins. Machine stitch down the lines to quilt the piece. (Alternatively, use a seam guide on your sewing machine.)

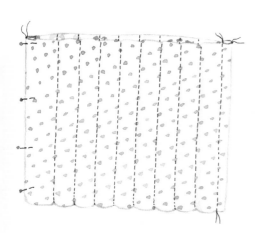

11 Lay the piece on a flat surface, with the lining facing upward. Fold it in half lengthwise, so the patchwork side faces upward. Pin and machine stitch down each side, using a ⅜-in. (1-cm) seam. Trim the seam allowances to ¼ in. (6 mm). Trim the corners. Turn the patchwork to the inside. Press the seams flat.

12 Pin and stitch along the side edges ⅜ in. (1 cm) from the edge. Turn the bag right side out.

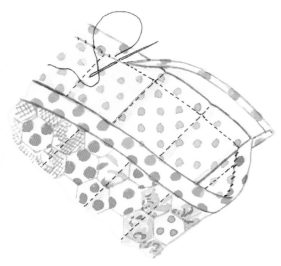

13 Trim the top edge of the bag so that it's straight. Measure around the top of the bag and cut the binding fabric to size—approx. 1¼ in./ 3 cm wide x the length (29½ in./75.5cm), plus an extra 1½ in. (4 cm) on the length for the seam. Fold each short end of the binding in by approx. ⅜ in. (1 cm) and press. Bind the top of the bag, following the instructions on page 138.

14 Attach the bag handles.

drawstring bag

This is a fun, simple project for anyone who is just starting out in patchwork. Choose your fabrics and trimmings carefully: I went through four or five different color combinations before reaching this one. Use it as a swimming bag, school bag, or laundry bag; it's so pretty and bright, there's no chance of you losing it!

YOU WILL NEED

Approx. twelve 4 x 18-in. (10 x 45.5-cm) strips of fabric for the patchwork

Two 23 x 16-in. (58.5 x 40.5-cm) pieces of cotton fabric for the backing

Two 32 x 1½-in. (80 x 4-cm) strips for the drawstring ties

10 4 x 18-in. (10 x 45.5-cm) lengths of decorative trim

finished size:

Approx. 19¼ x 14¼ in. (49 x 36 cm)

1 Press the patchwork fabrics and cut into strips approx. 4 in. (10 cm) wide and 18 in. (45.5 cm) in length. Lay the pieces out on the first piece of backing fabric in your chosen order, placing them at interesting angles to create a more dynamic effect.. Take a photo, make a quick sketch, or label the fabrics for reference.

2 Place the first piece of backing fabric right side down on your work surface. Pin the bottom edge of the first strip right side down along the top edge (you can angle it if you wish to make a more dynamic design). Machine stitch as close to the pinned edge as possible.

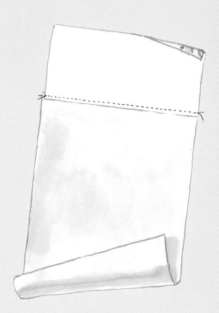

3 Fold the strip back along the stitching line, so that it's right side up, and press.

4 With right sides together, pin another strip on top of the unstitched edge of the first one and machine stitch them together, making sure your stitching goes through both layers. Continue layering strips of fabric over each other in this way until the whole backing fabric is covered.

5 Repeat steps 2–4 using the second piece of backing fabric.

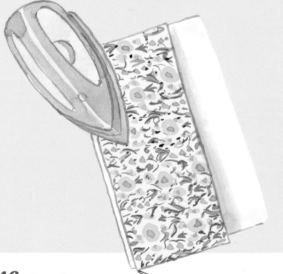

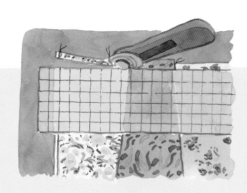

6 Trim the edges of both pieces straight.

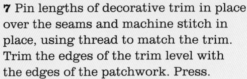

7 Pin lengths of decorative trim in place over the seams and machine stitch in place, using thread to match the trim. Trim the edges of the trim level with the edges of the patchwork. Press.

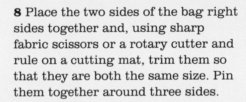

8 Place the two sides of the bag right sides together and, using sharp fabric scissors or a rotary cutter and rule on a cutting mat, trim them so that they are both the same size. Pin them together around three sides.

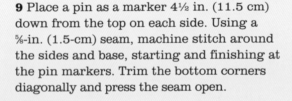

9 Place a pin as a marker 4½ in. (11.5 cm) down from the top on each side. Using a ⅝-in. (1.5-cm) seam, machine stitch around the sides and base, starting and finishing at the pin markers. Trim the bottom corners diagonally and press the seam open.

10 Press the unstitched section at the top of each side along the seam allowance. Turn the top edge over by ⅝ in. (1.5 cm) and press.

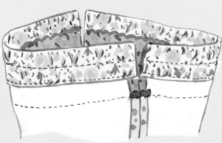

11 Press each top edge over to the wrong side by a further 2 in. (5 cm) and pin. Machine stitch the top hems in place with two parallel rows of stitching, one close to the first pressed edge and the second 1 in. (2.5 cm) above it to form two channels for the drawstrings.

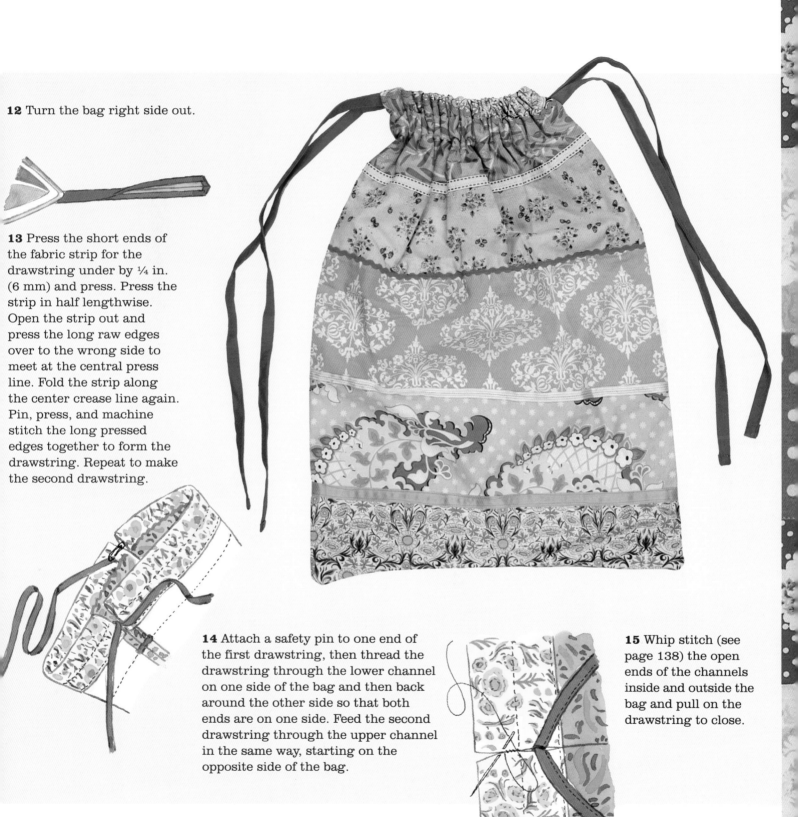

12 Turn the bag right side out.

13 Press the short ends of the fabric strip for the drawstring under by ¼ in. (6 mm) and press. Press the strip in half lengthwise. Open the strip out and press the long raw edges over to the wrong side to meet at the central press line. Fold the strip along the center crease line again. Pin, press, and machine stitch the long pressed edges together to form the drawstring. Repeat to make the second drawstring.

14 Attach a safety pin to one end of the first drawstring, then thread the drawstring through the lower channel on one side of the bag and then back around the other side so that both ends are on one side. Feed the second drawstring through the upper channel in the same way, starting on the opposite side of the bag.

15 Whip stitch (see page 138) the open ends of the channels inside and outside the bag and pull on the drawstring to close.

quilted bag
with metal clasp

OU WILL NEED

elve 3 x 16-in. (7 x 40-cm) strips of
tton fabric for patchwork

in. (50 cm) batting (wadding)

mplate on page 140

in. (50 cm) lining fabric

prox. 30 x 1 in. (75 x 2.5 cm) bias-
t fabric for strap

etal bag clasp

ished size

prox. 10½ x 12 in. (27 x 30.5 cm)

This just proves you can quilt a sophisticated bag! Here I've used some light and bright fabrics – but try using dark reds or velvets to make a more glamorous evening bag and a light chain handle instead of fabric to add a little more sophistication. I quilted in straight lines, but this is a great little project for trying out different quilted lines and shapes.

1 With right sides facing, using a ¼-in. (6-mm) seam, machine stitch six strips together along their long edges for the front of the bag. Press the seams open, turn over, and press the patchwork again on the right side. Repeat to make the patchwork for the back of the bag.

2 Cut two pieces of batting (wadding) the same size as the front and back of the bag. Lay each patchwork piece right side up on a piece of batting (wadding) and pin well to hold in place. Using black thread, machine stitch lines ¾ in. (2 cm) apart along both the front and back pieces. Remove the pins.

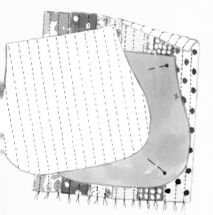

3 Enlarge the template on page 139 by 200 percent and cut out. Pin the template on top of the patchwork for the front of the bag and cut out. Repeat for the back of the bag.

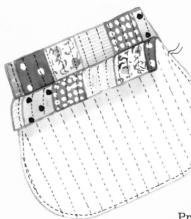

4 Using tailor's chalk, transfer the marks that indicate the start and finish of the stitching from the template to the front and back of the bag. With right sides together, using a neutral color of thread and a ¼-in. (6-mm) seam, machine stitch the front piece to the back between the marked points. Press the seam open. Turn the bag right side out.

5 Repeat steps 3 and 4 with the lining fabric, but do not turn right side out.

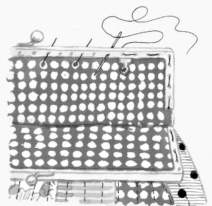

6 Insert the lining into the bag, with the wrong side of the lining facing the wrong side of the bag. Pin and machine stitch the lining to the bag along the top edge, close to the edge.

7 Turn the open side edges of both the lining and the patchwork pieces under by ¼ in. (6 mm) and press. Place the clasp on the inside of the bag and ease the top edge of the fabric into it. Using doubled sewing thread, hand stitch the clasp in place along all edges by stitching through the holes in the clasp and into the fabric. It's useful to place pins through the bag and into the holes in the clasp to keep the fabric in position while sewing.

8 Fold the strap in half lengthwise, right sides together. Pin and machine stitch along the length, close to the edge. Turn the strap right side out, using a safety pin or knitting needle.

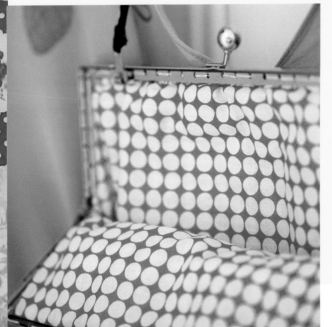

9 Thread the strap through the tie catches on the clasp, fold the ends under, and hand stitch neatly in place.

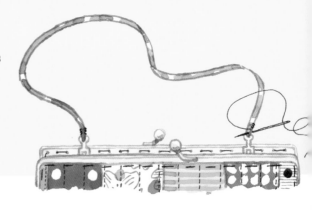

sewing purse

This is a great portable sewing case—small and perfect for keeping spare feet (the sewing machine kind), threads, bobbins, scissors, tailor's chalk, and tape measures. You'll be amazed at how much it can hold—it's a real Mary Poppins bag!

YOU WILL NEED

18 x 6½ in. (46 x 17 cm) cotton print fabric for main piece

18 x 6½ in. (46 x 17 cm) cotton print fabric for lining

20 x 9 in. (51 x 23 cm) batting (wadding)

Two 3 x 6½-in. (7.5 x 17-cm), one 3¼ x 6½-in. (8.5 x 17-cm), and one 4¼ x 6½-in. (11 x 17-cm) pieces of cotton fabric in different patterned fabrics for pockets

Two 3 x 6½-in. (7.5 x 17-cm), one 3¼ x 6½-in. (8.5 x 17-cm), and one 4¼ x 6½-in. (11 x 17-cm) pieces of cotton fabric for pocket linings

Two 3 x 6½-in. (7.5 x 17-cm), one 3¼ x 6½-in. (8.5 x 17-cm), and one 4¼ x 6½-in. (11 x 17-cm) pieces of batting (wadding) for pockets

Four 2½ x 6½-in. (6 x 17 cm) bias-cut strips to bind the pockets

60 in. (1.5 m) bias-cut fabric, 2½ in. (6 cm) wide, for binding

39 in. (1 m) ribbon, ⅝ in. (1.5 cm) wide, for ties

finished size:

6¼ x 4¾ in. (16 x 12 cm)

1 Place the main piece and lining on top of each other. Place a plate over the corners of one short end, as shown, draw around it, and cut along the drawn line to round off the corners.

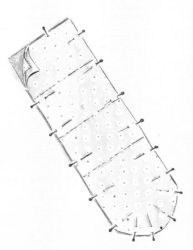

2 Draw lines across the lining fabric on the right side 3¾, 7½, and 11¼ in. (9.5, 19, and 28.5 cm) up from the bottom straight edge. Fold the lining in half lengthwise and mark the center point on the curved end.

3 Place the batting (wadding) on a flat surface with the lining right side up on top. Pin well. Trim the batting level with the lining. Turn the piece over and pin the main piece to the batting, right side up, making sure that the rounded corners of all three layers align.

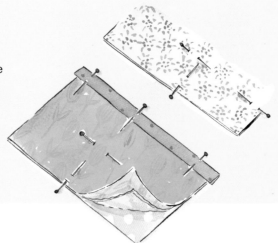

4 Now make the pockets (make all four in the same way). Place the pocket lining right side down on a flat surface with the batting (wadding) on top and the pocket fabric right side up on top of the batting. Pin well. Bind the top edge of each pocket, following the instructions on page 138.

5 Pin one of the 3 x 6½-in. (7.5 x 17-cm) pockets right side up on the bottom edge of the lining. Using a ¼-in. (6-mm) seam, machine stitch around the bottom and sides of the pocket.

6 Right sides together, pin the second 3 x 6½-in. (7.5 x 17-cm) pocket on top of the first one, aligning the raw edge with the first marked line on the lining. Machine stitch ¼ in. (6 mm) below the raw edge. Fold the pocket up along the stitching line so that the binding is at the top. Machine stitch ¼ in. (6 mm) above the stitching line. Using a ¼-in. (6-mm) seam, pin and sew the sides to secure the pocket in place.

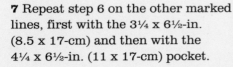

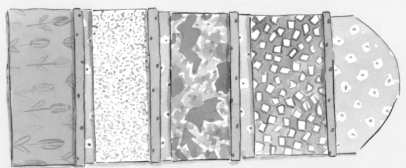

7 Repeat step 6 on the other marked lines, first with the 3¼ x 6½-in. (8.5 x 17-cm) and then with the 4¼ x 6½-in. (11 x 17-cm) pocket.

8 Using either ready-made or your own bias binding, bind the edges of the purse (see page 138), mitering the corners.

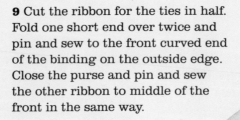

9 Cut the ribbon for the ties in half. Fold one short end over twice and pin and sew to the front curved end of the binding on the outside edge. Close the purse and pin and sew the other ribbon to middle of the front in the same way.

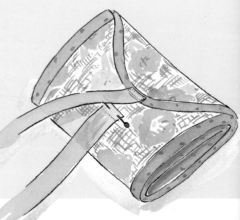

flower coin purse

This is a really quick-and-easy project and makes a lovely gift. The appliqué flower is a great way of using up pretty fabric scraps.

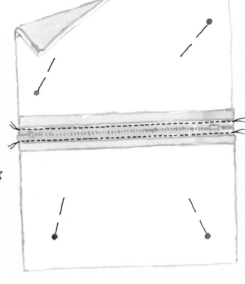

YOU WILL NEED

Two 8 x 5½-in. (20 x 14-cm) pieces of cotton print fabric for main piece

Two 8 x 5½-in. (20 x 14-cm) pieces of cotton print fabric for lining

Two 8 x 5½-in. (20 x 14-cm) pieces of batting (wadding)

6 in. (15 cm) zipper

Paper-backed fusible bonding web

Assorted fabric scraps for petals and flower center

Templates on page 140

Contrasting decorative thread

finished size:
7½ x 5 in. (19 x 13 cm)

1 Pin a piece of batting (wadding) to the wrong side of each main fabric piece. Pin the two main fabric pieces right sides together. Fold each top edge over by ⅝ in. (1.5 cm) and press. Insert the zipper, following the instructions on page 129.

2 Trace the templates on page 140 onto card and cut out. Following the instructions on page 132, iron small pieces of paper-backed fusible bonding web onto the wrong side of your chosen appliqué fabrics. Draw around the templates on the wrong side of the fabric and cut out ten petals and two flower centers.

3 Apply the petals to the front of the purse, following the instructions on page 132. Zigzag stitch around each petal in a contrasting color of thread. Apply the flower centers in the same way. Repeat the appliqué on the back of the purse.

4 Open the zipper. With right sides together, using a ¼-in. (6-mm) seam, pin the sides and bottom of the purse together and machine stitch. Trim the corners and seam allowances.

5 With right sides together, using a ¼-in. (6-mm) seam, pin and machine stitch the sides and bottom of the lining pieces together. Remove the pins, trim the corners, and press open the seams. Fold the top edge over to the wrong side by ⅝ in. (1.5 cm) and press.

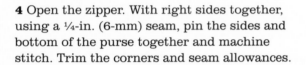

6 Turn the main piece inside out and fit the lining over it, wrong sides to wrong sides. Pin and hand stitch the lining to the top edge of the main piece. Turn right side out and press.

make-up bag

You can never have enough make-up bags! This is a good opportunity to practice your sewing-machine skills and appliqué circles. The bag has a flat bottom, and is the perfect size for all your cosmetic bits and pieces. It takes very little fabric and is a great project for using up scraps; the chances are that the only thing you'll need to buy is a zipper.

level: intermediate

YOU WILL NEED

Two 10 x 7-in. (26 x 18-cm) pieces of main fabric

7-in. (18-cm) zipper

Two 10 x 7-in. (26 x 18-cm) pieces of batting (wadding)

23 in. (59 cm) light blue rick-rack braid

Two 10 x 7-in. (26 x 18-cm) pieces of lining fabric

Fabric scraps for circles approx. 1¼ in. (3 cm) in diameter

Fusible bonding web

finished size:

9 x 5 in. (24 x 13 cm)

1 Place the two main fabric pieces right sides together. Following the instructions on page 129, insert a centered zipper.

2 Pin a piece of batting (wadding) to the wrong side of each main piece, aligning it with the raw edges.

3 Place rick-rack braid ¾ in. (2 cm) down from the top edge, 2¼ in. (5.5 cm) from the bottom edge, and 1¼ in. (3 cm) in from the sides to create a frame. Pin and machine stitch in place.

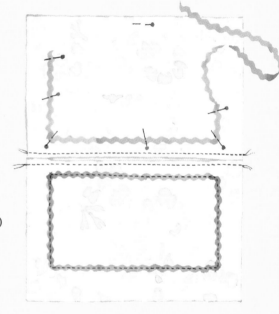

4 Following the manufacturer's instructions, iron fusible bonding web to the wrong side of your chosen fabric scraps and cut circles approx. 1¼ in. (3 cm) in diameter. Place the circles inside the rick-rack frame, pin in place and apply (see page 132). Zig-zag stitch around all the circles.

make-up bag **59**

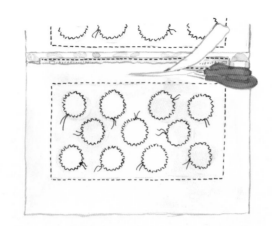

5 Trim the batting (wadding) level with the main fabric around the edges and just below the zipper.

6 leaving the zipper open and with right sides together, using a ⅝-in. (1.5-cm) seam, pin and machine stitch the side and bottom seams of the bag.

7 Tweak the fabric until the side seam is directly over the base seam in one corner, then pin across the corner to hold the layers together. Place the bag on a flat surface and measure 1 in. (2.5 cm) down the seam line from the corner; draw a line across the corner at this point. Pin and machine stitch along the line. Repeat on the other corner, then trim both corner seams diagonally about ¼ in. (6 mm) beyond the stitching.

8 With right sides together, using a ⅝-in. (1.5-cm) seam, pin and machine stitch the side and bottom seams of the lining, leaving the top open. Press all seams open. Repeat step 7 to make the corners in the same way as for the main piece.

9 Fold the top edge of the lining over to the wrong side by ⅝ in. (1.5 cm) and press.

10 Slip the lining over the main piece, wrong side to wrong side. Pin the lining to the main bag and whip stitch in place (see page 138). Turn the bag right side out.

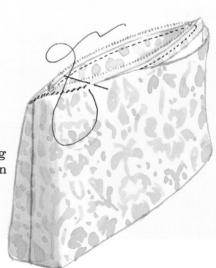

Yo-yo purse

Yo-yos are perfect little projects to make while watching television. This purse is just the right size for your phone, money, and lipstick. Use scraps of nine or ten different fabrics for the yo-yos. The outside fabric of the purse can be made in a plain, neutral color, but choose something pretty that contrasts well with the colors of the yo-yos for the lining.

1 Enlarge the template on page 141 by 200 percent and cut out. Cut one front and one back from the main fabric, and one front and one back from the lining fabric. Transfer the marks on the template to all fabric pieces.

level: intermediate

YOU WILL NEED

Template on page 141

10 x 10 in. (26 x 26 cm) light-colored main fabric

10 x 10 in. (26 x 26 cm) lining fabric

Metal bag clasp 5 in. (13 cm) wide

Approx. 60 circles of fabric, 2½ in. (6 cm) in diameter, for the yo-yos

finished size:

Approx. 7 x 6 in. (17.5 x 15 cm)

2 Pin the front and back main pieces right sides together. Starting at the marked points, using a ¼-in. (6-mm) seam, machine stitch the pieces together. Repeat with the front and back lining pieces. Press open the seams. Turn the main piece right side out, but leave the lining wrong side out.

3 Insert the lining into the purse, wrong sides to wrong sides. Machine stitch the lining to the main piece along the top edge, stitching close to the edge.

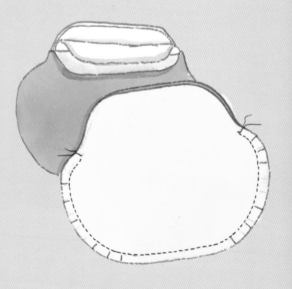

4 Turn the open side edges under by ¼ in. (6 mm) and press. Place the clasp on the inside of the bag and ease the top edge of the fabric into it. Using doubled sewing thread, hand stitch the clasp in place along all edges by stitching through the holes in the clasp and into the fabric. It's useful to place pins through the bag and into the holes in the clasp to keep the fabric in position while sewing.

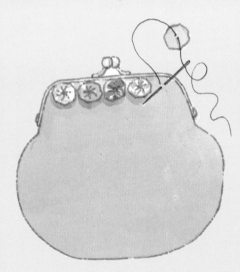

5 Make the yo-yos, following the instructions on page 131. Hand stitch yo-yos onto the back and front of purse, placing them close together and taking care to stitch through the main fabric only, not the lining fabric.

laptop cover

YOU WILL NEED

Assorted fabric scraps for patchwork (approx. 30 in./75 cm in total)

Approx. 20 in. (50 cm) lining fabric

Approx. 20 in. (50 cm) batting (wadding)

20 in. (50 cm) ribbon, ½ in. (15 mm) wide, for ties

I work from my laptop and am guilty of leaving it open to gather dust. This quilted patchwork cover not only protects it, but also gives me something gorgeous to look at. I had scraps of the most beautiful fabrics that were much too nice to keep hidden away, so this was the perfect chance to use them up.

1 Make the lining first, so you can use it as a template for the patchwork. With right sides together, using a ⅝-in. (1.5-cm) seam, pin and machine stitch the side and bottom seams. Put the laptop into the lining to check the fit. If it's too large at the sides, stitch it again to make it smaller until the laptop fits snugly inside the lining. Cut two pieces of batting (wadding) the same size as the lining.

measuring and cutting

Laptops come in different sizes, so follow the instructions below to work out exactly how big your fabric pieces need to be.

lining

First, measure the width and length of your laptop. Add 1¼ in. (3 cm) to the width for the side seam allowances. Then add ⅝ in. (1.5 cm) for the bottom seam allowance plus 1 in. (2.5 cm) for the top hem to the length. Now measure the depth of your laptop and add this measurement to each edge. Cut two pieces of lining fabric to this size.

patchwork

The patchwork is made up of pieces that, when stitched, are 1¼ in. (3 cm) square. To work out how many squares and rows you will need, divide the length and width of the lining fabric by 1¼ in. (3 cm); this allows for all the seam allowances and the top hem. This gives you the number of squares required for one side of the cover; double it to work out the number of squares needed to make both the top and bottom. Use the lining as a template to check that your finished patchwork is the right size; you can add more squares if necessary (see step 5).

2 Now make the patchwork. Cut strips of fabric 1¾ in. (4.5 cm) wide; the length will depend on the layout of colors. Then cut the strips into squares; you can cut more than one strip at a time by stacking the strips. Lay the squares out in your chosen design for each side of the cover and label the rows (see page 130).

3 Join the squares for the top of the cover together in rows, using a ¼-in. (6-mm) seam. Press the seams to one side, all in the same direction. Press again on the right side.

4 Pin the rows together at the joins of the squares, and machine stitch, using a ¼-in. (6-mm) seam. Press the seams to one side, all in the same direction. Press the patchwork on both sides. Repeat steps 2–4 to make the patchwork for the bottom of the cover.

5 Check that the patchwork is big enough to cover your laptop, allowing extra for the seam allowances (see box on page 65). If it is too small, add more rows. Measure the patchwork against the lining to make sure it is the same size.

6 Lay the patchwork right side up on top of the batting (wadding), smooth out, and pin well. Using a walking foot if you have one, and a contrasting color of thread, machine stitch a diagonal line from one corner to the other. When all the squares have one diagonal line sewn through them, sew diagonal lines from the opposite direction, so that all squares have a cross sewn through them.

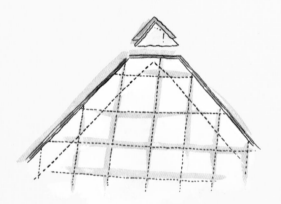

7 With right sides together, using a ⅝-in. (1.5-cm) seam, pin and machine stitch the side and bottom edges. Trim the bottom corners and press the seam open. Turn the patchwork right side out.

8 Fold the top edge in by approx. 1 in. (2.5 cm) and pin in place. Check the size at this point by placing your laptop in the cover; if necessary, adjust the depth of the top hem.

9 Trim the bottom corners of the lining and press the seam open. Ease the lining into the patchwork cover, aligning the seams and smoothing it out so that it fits well and there are no creases. Pinning the bottom corners of the lining and patchwork together will make this easier.

10 Fold the top of the lining in toward the patchwork, so that both folded edges meet. Pin in place. Take out the pins that are holding the top of the patchwork. Machine stitch along the top close to the edge, using a matching color of thread (or a neutral color if you are using multicolored fabrics). Take out the pins. Press.

11 Whip stitch the top edge of lining in place (see page 138) for a really neat finish.

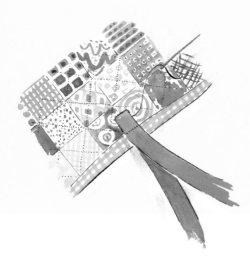

12 Cut the ribbon for the ties in half. Fold one raw edge of the ribbon under by approx ¼ in. (6 mm) and pin it to the center of the top of the cover. Repeat on the other side.

feedsack bag

YOU WILL NEED

Approx. 20 in. (50 cm) each of seven fabrics for the log cabin design

Two 2 x 13-in. (5 x 33-cm) strips of fabric for the top band

13 x 13 in. (33 x 33 cm) fabric for lining

13 x 13 in. (33 x 33 cm) batting (wadding)

Four 2½ x 20-in. (6 x 50-cm) strips for handles

Finished size

11½ x 12 in. (29 x 30.5 cm)

During the Great Depression of the 1920s and 30s in the US, many feedsacks had colorful logos and women realized that they could be used as fabric for quilts and garments. This bag is made using reproduction feedsack fabrics. The design is known as Courthouse Steps, a variation on the traditional Log Cabin. Here, however, I've used only two squares in the center instead of the more usual three, and placed the colors randomly rather than having light tones on two opposite sides of the block and dark tones on the other two sides.

1 Cut strips of fabric 2 in. (5 cm) wide. These will be added from the center outward to make the block, so will range in length from 2 in. (5 cm) at the center to approx 12½ in. (32 cm) at the outer edges. Decide—roughly—on the arrangement of the strips in the block.

2 Take one of the fabrics that will be at the center of the block and cut across it at right angles to a length of 2 in. (5 cm), giving a 2-in. (5-cm) square. Cut the second center square in a different fabric in the same way.

3 Pin the two squares right sides together and, using a ¼-in. (6-mm) foot on the machine, join them on one side with a ¼-in. (6-mm) seam. Press the seam to one side.

4 Pin another length of fabric right sides together along one long edge of the pressed unit and attach it in the same way. Trim the edge level with the first pressed unit after sewing. Press the seam to one side.

stitch advice

Accurate measuring and sewing are important in this design to ensure that the front and back are the same size. Use a rotary cutter and take your time.

5 Repeat step 4, adding another strip to the opposite long edge of the pressed unit.

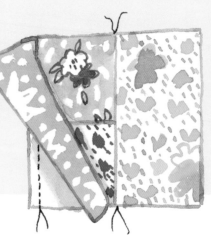

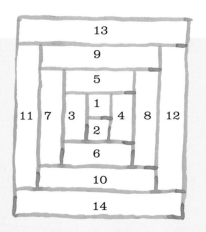

6 Continue adding pieces in the order shown—to opposite sides of the central pieced unit, then to the top and bottom. This creates a design than is slightly taller than it is wide. If you want to make the bag wider, so that it is almost square, add extra strip(s) to the side or sides as we have done here; if you want to make it taller still, add extra strip(s) to the top and/or bottom.

7 Repeat steps 1–6 to make a second Courthouse Steps block. When you have completed both blocks, press and place on the cutting mat and trim so that the front and back measure the same. Turn over and press both pieces on right side.

8 Cut two pieces of batting (wadding) ½ in. (1 cm) larger all around than the front and back pieces. Lay the back and front on the batting (wadding), right side up, and pin in place. With a contrasting color of thread, machine stitch lines horizontally across the strips approx. 1 in. (2.5 cm) apart. Press and remove the pins.

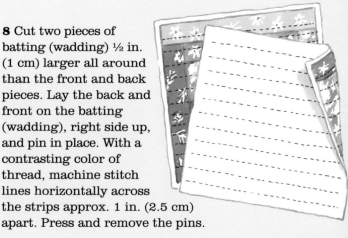

9 Cut two pieces for the top bands measuring the width of the front and back pieces by 2 in. (5 cm). With right sides together, pin each top band to the top of a main piece. Machine stitch, using a ¼-in. (6-mm) seam. Press the seam to one side.

10 Pin the front and back pieces right sides together and machine stitch along the side and bottom edges, using a ¼-in. (6-mm) seam and leaving the top edge open. Trim the bottom corners diagonally and press the seam open.

11 Turn the top band over to the inside of the bag by about ¾ in. (2 cm); it should just cover the batting (wadding). Press well. Turn the bag right side out.

12 Cut two pieces of lining fabric the same size as the front and back pieces. Pin them right sides together and machine stitch along the side and bottom edges, using a ¼-in. (6-mm) seam and leaving the top edge open. Trim the bottom corners diagonally and press the seam open.

13 Slip the lining inside the bag and ease it right down into the corners and sides. Fold the lining fabric over at the top to match the top of the bag, pin in place, and press along the top edge.

14 Fold the long edges of each handle in to meet in the center. Press. Place two handle pieces wrong sides together. Pin and machine stitch down each edge, as close to the edge as possible. Repeat with the other pair of handles.

15 Place a pin marker 2 in. (5 cm) from the outside edges on each side of the bag. Slip each end of the first handle between the lining and the main piece at the marked points on one side of the bag, with the ends of the handle 1½ in. (4 cm) from the top of the bag. Repeat on the other side of the bag with the other handle.

16 Stitch around the top edge of the bag as close to the edge as possible, incorporating the handles. Reinforce each end of each handle by stitching a criss-cross square on the outside top of the bag where the handles have been fitted. Press the top edge.

accessories & gifts

patchwork picture

YOU WILL NEED

Two pieces of contrasting fabric for the background

Batting (wadding)

Fabric scraps for the picture

Templates on page 141

Fabric spray adhesive

Frame

You can either use the templates on page 141 to make this picture or cut out shapes to make your own house and accessories—a great chance to be creative. This picture was made to fit into an 18 x 16-in. (45.5 x 40.5-cm) frame, but you can make yours to fit any frame size.

1 Right sides together, machine stitch the two pieces of background fabric together horizontally to make a piece approx. 2 in. (5 cm) all around bigger than your frame. The "sky" area should make up roughly the top two-thirds of the piece and the "ground" the bottom third. Press open the seam, then press the piece well from the front. Cut a piece of batting (wadding) to the same size.

2 Enlarge the templates on page 141 by 200 percent and cut out. Pin the paper templates to the fabrics of your choice and cut out the individual picture pieces.

3 Using the window mount from the frame as a guide, mark out the area of your picture on the background fabric. Spray the back of each picture piece with fabric adhesive and place on the background fabric. Place the picture on top of the wadding (batting) and pin the layers together.

5 Embroider eyes, feathers, and feet on the hens, a trailing string for the kite, and three flying birds in the sky. Cut out three pairs of very small triangles, place in position along the kite string, and stitch in place.

4 Put the piece in an embroidery hoop, if you have one, and freehand machine embroider the motifs, using two lines to outline each piece. Embroider a cross on each window for the glazing bars, a letterbox and handle on the door, spirals in the roses, and stems beneath the roses.

6 When all pieces are stitched in place, trim all loose ends of thread and press the picture well. Trim the edges to fit inside the picture frame. Spray fabric adhesive on the back to attach the piece to the hardboard of the picture frame and insert into the frame.

needle case

This is a beautiful addition to any sewing box. I made one for each of my children and embroidered their initial on the front instead of the daisy.

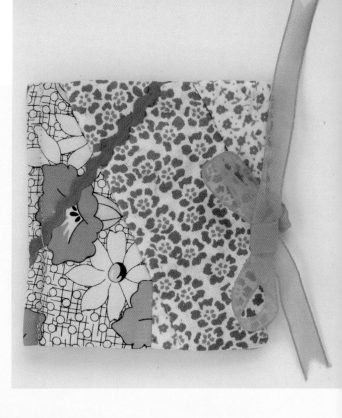

level: beginner

YOU WILL NEED

5 or 6 small strips of cotton print fabrics for the front of the needle case

8 x 5 in. (20 x 12 cm) white or neutral cotton fabric for backing

7 x 4 in. (18 x 10 cm) green felt for lining

Approx. 8 in. (20 cm) ribbon or rick-rack braid

Fabric scraps for the appliqué

Templates on page 141

Embroidery floss (thread)

Organza ribbon, approx ¼ in. (6 mm) wide

7 x 4 in. (18 x 10 cm), white felt for the "pages" of the needle case

finished size:
3¾ x 3½ in. (9 x 9.5 cm)

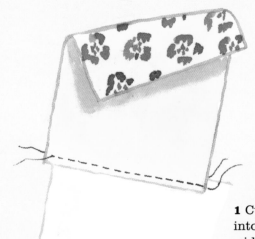

1 Cut the fabric for the front of the needle case into strips between 1 and 2 in. (2.5 and 5 cm) wide. Place the backing fabric right side down on your work surface. Pin the bottom edge of the first strip right side down along the top edge (you can angle it if you wish to make a more dynamic design). Machine stitch as close to the pinned edge as possible.

2 Fold the strip back along the stitching line, so that it's right side up, and press.

3 With right sides together, pin another strip on top of the unstitched edge of the first piece and machine stitch them together, making sure your stitching goes through both layers. Fold the second strip back along the stitching line as before, and press.

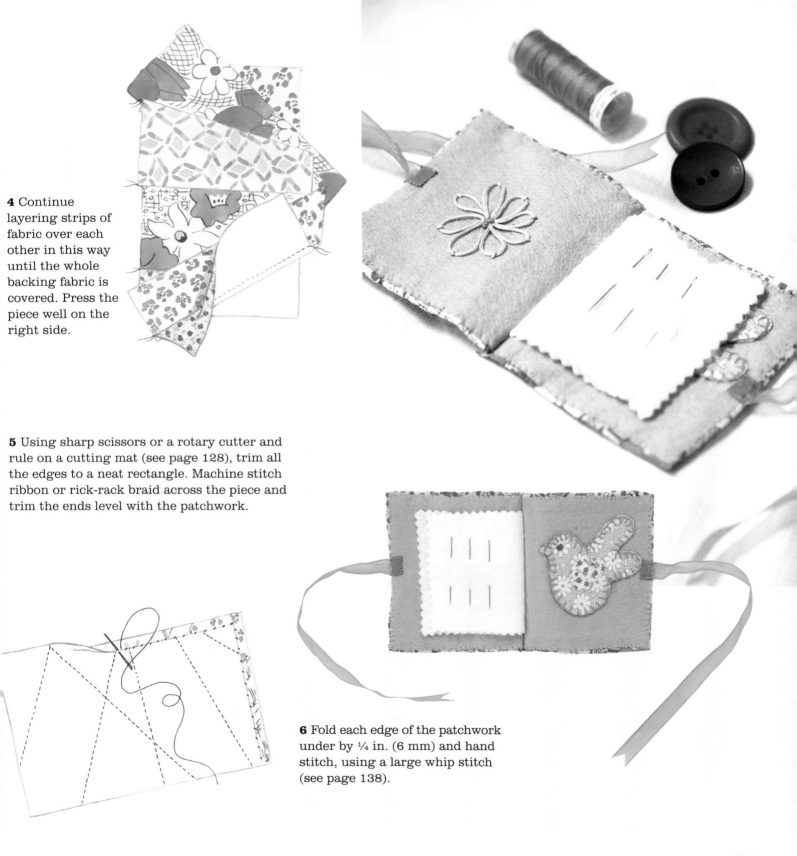

4 Continue layering strips of fabric over each other in this way until the whole backing fabric is covered. Press the piece well on the right side.

5 Using sharp scissors or a rotary cutter and rule on a cutting mat (see page 128), trim all the edges to a neat rectangle. Machine stitch ribbon or rick-rack braid across the piece and trim the ends level with the patchwork.

6 Fold each edge of the patchwork under by ¼ in. (6 mm) and hand stitch, using a large whip stitch (see page 138).

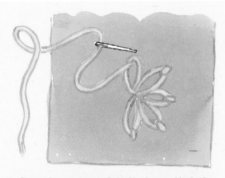

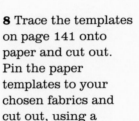

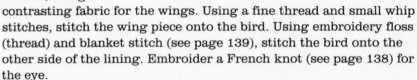

7 Cut the green felt lining slightly smaller all around than the patchwork. Using detached chain stitch (see page 139), embroider a daisy on one side of the lining.

8 Trace the templates on page 141 onto paper and cut out. Pin the paper templates to your chosen fabrics and cut out, using a contrasting fabric for the wings. Using a fine thread and small whip stitches, stitch the wing piece onto the bird. Using embroidery floss (thread) and blanket stitch (see page 139), stitch the bird onto the other side of the lining. Embroider a French knot (see page 138) for the eye.

9 Center a length of ribbon on each side of the inside of the case and pin in place. Hand stitch the green felt lining to the wrong side of the patchwork, using small, neat whip stitches (see page 138).

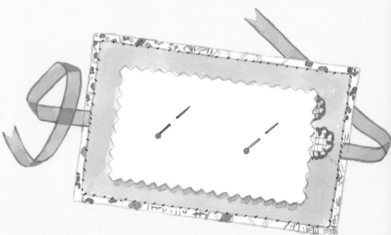

10 Using pinking shears, cut a 5½ x 3-in. (14 x 7.5-cm) piece of white felt for the inner piece. Center it on top of the green felt lining and pin in place. With wrong sides together, fold the case in half widthwise and press. On right side, machine stitch along the "spine" of the case, ½ in. (1.5 cm) from the fold. Remove the pins.

book cover

I left my gardening book in the greenhouse for so long that the cover began to perish, so this is the perfect replacement for it—and it looks pretty, too. It would also make a beautiful cover for a wedding or baby album.

1 Use the dust jacket of the book as your template, if it has one. If it doesn't, make your own from paper or thin cardstock: for the front/back cover template, open out the book, measure the height and the width, and add an extra ¾ in. (2 cm) all around. Make a separate template for the flaps, again adding an extra ¾ in. (2 cm) all around.

2 Pin the front/back cover template to the main fabric, and the flap template to the contrasting fabric. Cut one front/back cover and two flaps.

3 Cut the ribbon for the ties in half. Pin one length of ribbon to the center of the right-hand edge of the front/back piece. With right sides together, place a flap on top aligning the edges. Pin in place and machine stitch, using a 5/8-in. (1.5-cm) seam and making sure you catch the ribbon in the stitching. Press the seam open.

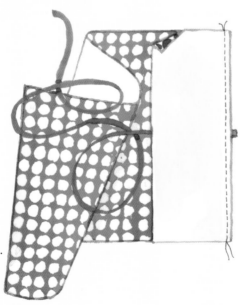

level: experienced

YOU WILL NEED

Fabric 1 (front/back): cotton print fabric

Fabric 2 (flaps): contrasting cotton print fabric

White cotton fabric for lining

Batting (wadding)

39 in. (1 m) ribbon, ½ in. (12 mm) wide, for ties

Hexagon template on page 139

Scraps of assorted fabrics for the hexagon "flowers"

fabric quantities

The amount of fabric for this project depends on the size of the book you are covering; see step 1 for details of how to work out how much you need.

4 Attach the second flap to the other short end of the front/back piece in the same way, this time without incorporating a ribbon in the seam. Stitch down each seam on the right side.

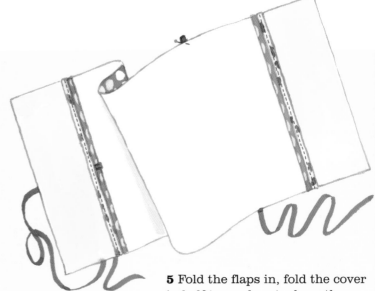

5 Fold the flaps in, fold the cover in half to work out where the center top edge of the back cover will be, and lightly mark this point. Open the cover out again and place one end of the remaining length of ribbon at this point on the right side. Pin, then machine stitch in place.

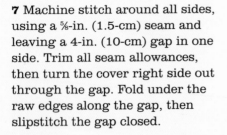

6 Cut the lining fabric and batting (wadding) to the same size as the book cover. Place the batting (wadding) on a flat surface, with the lining fabric right side up on top, and the cover right side down on top of the lining. Pin the layers together.

7 Machine stitch around all sides, using a ⅝-in. (1.5-cm) seam and leaving a 4-in. (10-cm) gap in one side. Trim all seam allowances, then turn the cover right side out through the gap. Fold under the raw edges along the gap, then slipstitch the gap closed.

8 Fold the flaps over to the inside and whip stitch along the top and bottom edges (see page 138).

9 Following the instructions on page 43, make a hexagon "flower" with two rows of hexagons around the center and slipstitch it to the front of the cover.

trip around the world pillow

A Trip Around the World is a traditional patchwork design of small squares in diagonal lines. I've used bold blacks, reds, yellows, and blues to make the pillow look contemporary and crisp.

YOU WILL NEED

49 x 2¼-in. (6-cm) squares in five cotton prints for the patchwork (see step 1)

Two 3 x 13¾-in. (8 x 35-cm) and two 3 x 19-in. (8 x 48-cm) strips of cotton print fabric for the front panels

19-in. (48-cm) square of cotton print fabric for the back panel

18-in. (45-cm) pillow form (cushion pad)

finished size:

18 x 18 in. (45 x 45 cm)

1 Cut strips of each fabric, 2¼ in. (6 cm) wide. Using a rotary cutter and rule on a cutting mat, cut each strip into the required number of 2¼-in. (6-cm) squares. You will need one center square (fabric A), four of fabric B, eight of fabric C, 12 of fabric D, and 24 of fabric E. Starting from the center and working outward, arrange the squares as shown.

2 Using a ¼-in. (6-mm) seam and a shorter than normal stitch, join the squares in each horizontal row together. There is no need to pin, but do make sure the squares are correctly aligned. Press the seams in alternate rows in opposite directions—row 1 to the left, row 2 to the right, and so on.

3 Pin the rows together at the joins of the squares and sew using a ¼ in (6-mm) seam. Press the seams in alternate rows in opposite directions.

4 Using a rotary cutter and rule on a cutting mat (see page 128), trim the block to 12½ in. (32 cm) square.

5 With right sides together, using a ⅝-in. (1.5-cm) seam, machine stitch the shorter strips of fabric to opposite sides of the patchwork panel; attach the longer strips to the top and bottom of the patchwork panel in the same way. Press the seams open. Trim the front to 19 in. (48 cm) square.

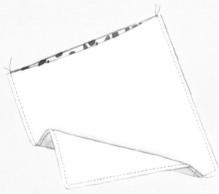

6 With right sides facing, pin the back piece to the completed front panel. Using a ⅝-in. (1.5-cm) seam, machine stitch around three sides. Trim the corners diagonally. Press the seams open, turn the cover right side out, and insert the pillow form (cushion pad).

7 Turn under the raw edges of the fourth side by ⅝ in. (1.5 cm) and press, then whip stitch the seam closed (see page 138).

The measurements for the strips that go around the center panel are based on a center panel measuring 13¾ in. (35 cm) square. If your panel is a different size, adjust the measurements as follows:

Pieces 1 and 2
Width: 19 in./48 cm minus the panel width, divided by two, plus ⅝ in. (1.5 cm) all around each piece
Length: center panel length

Pieces 3 and 4
Width: 19 in. (48 cm) minus the panel width, divided by two, plus ⅝ in. (1.5 cm) all around each piece
Length: 19 in. (48 cm)

blue pillow

This is a gorgeous way of putting lovely fabrics together. You need just six relatively small pieces of fabric, so you can easily make it out of scraps. I've chosen some interesting vintage buttons to match.

1 Cut all six pieces to size and label them to keep them in order. Pin pieces 1 and 2 right sides together along their width and machine stitch, with a 5/8-in. (1.5-cm) seam. Press the seam open. Repeat with pieces 3 and 4.

YOU WILL NEED

Piece 1: 10 x 11 in.
(26 x 28 cm) cotton fabric

Piece 2: 10 x 11 in.
(26 x 28 cm) cotton fabric

Piece 3: 11¾ x 9 in.
(32 x 24 cm) cotton fabric

Piece 4: 8¼ x 9 in.
(20 x 24 cm) cotton fabric

Piece 5: 19 x 11½ in.
(48 x 29 cm) cotton fabric

Piece 6: 19 x 12½ in.
(48 x 32.5 cm) cotton fabric

18 x 18-in. (45 x 45-cm)
pillow form (cushion pad)

3 buttons, approx. 1 in.
(2.5 cm) in diameter

finished size:
18 x 18 in. (45 x 45 cm)

2 Pin and machine stitch pieces 1 and 2 to pieces 3 and 4, making sure you keep them in order. These pieces form the front of the pillow.

3 Fold one 19-in. (48-cm) edge of piece 5 under by 2 in. (5 cm). Pin and press. Remove the pins and open out the fold. Fold the raw edge in to meet the press mark, then fold along the press line again and make a 1-in. (2.5-cm) hem. Pin, press, and machine stitch close to the edge. Repeat along one 19-in. (48-cm) edge of piece 6. These hemmed edges form the button bands.

4 Right sides down, pin the button band of piece 6 on top of the button band of piece 5. These two pieces form the back of the pillow.

5 With right sides together, pin the back and front of the pillow together. Machine stitch around all four sides with a ⅝-in. (1.5-cm) seam. Trim the corners diagonally. Press the seams open. Remove all pins and turn right side out.

6 Work three buttonholes on the top button band (see page 130), spacing them evenly, and hand sew buttons to the bottom button band to correspond.

vintage dish towel bunting

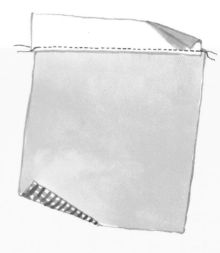

This bunting would look fantastic in a kitchen. It uses a crazy patchwork technique, where strips of fabric are layered over each other to give a random collage.

level: beginner

YOU WILL NEED

8–9 vintage dish towels in different styles and patterns

Nine x 12-in. (30-cm) squares of red gingham fabric for backing

128 in. (3.25 m) jumbo rick-rack, red

Template on page 140

finished size:

Length: approx. 94 in. (2.4 m); each flag is approx. 10½ in. (27 cm) tall

1 Cut the vintage dish towels into strips, varying in width between 2½ and 4½ in. (6.5 and 12 cm).

2 Place a gingham square right side down on your work surface. Pin the bottom edge of the first dish towel strip right side down along the top edge (you can angle it if you wish to make a more dynamic design). Machine stitch as close to the pinned edge as possible.

3 Fold the dish towel strip back along the stitching line, so that it's right side up, and press well along the seam.

4 With right sides together, pin another strip of dish towel on top of the first piece and machine stitch them together along the unstitched edge of the first piece, making sure your stitching goes through both layers. Fold the second strip back along the stitching line as before, so that it's right side up, and press.

5 Continue layering strips of fabric over each other until the whole backing fabric is covered. Place the strips at an angle to create a more interesting effect.

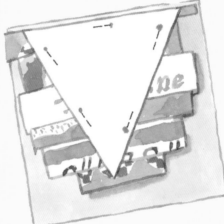

6 Enlarge the template on page 140 by 200 percent and cut out. Pin the template to the crazy patchwork and cut out a flag. Repeat steps 1–6 to make nine flags in total.

7 Turn up the bottom tip of each flag by about ¼ in. (6 mm) and press. Fold and press approx. ¼ in. (6 mm) to the wrong side along each side, making sure that the side edges meet at the tip to create a sharp point. Tuck the raw edges under, pin, and machine stitch. Trim the top edges. Press well.

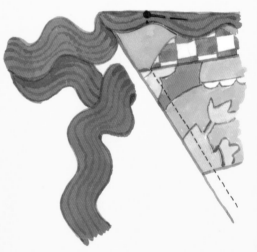

8 Leaving a 12-in. (30-cm) tail, pin the top of the first flag along the center of the rick-rack. Pin the remaining flags in place in the same way, butting them up against each other and leaving a 12-in. (30-cm) tail of rick-rack at the other end.

9 Fold the rick-rack over the tops of the flags to enclose the raw edges, pin it in place and whip stitch (see page 138) along the rick-rack to secure the flags in place.

bobble pillow

This is a really simple pillow to make and is an ideal introduction to patchwork, with gorgeous fabrics set against a clean, white background for the front panel.

1 Using a ready-made perspex square template and scissors or a rotary cutter and rule (see page 128), cut 16 x 4⅓-in. (11-cm) squares in fabrics of your choice; I cut two squares each of eight different fabrics. Lay them out on a flat surface and arrange them in four rows of four. Label the rows and the order of the squares (see page 130).

2 Right sides together, using ¼-in. (6-mm) seams and making sure you keep the squares in order, machine stitch the squares in each row together. Press the seams in each row to one side, all in the same direction.

3 Machine stitch the four rows together, again using ¼-in. (6-mm) seams. Press the seams to one side, all in the same direction. Fold all edges of the patchwork over to the wrong side by ¼ in. (6 mm). Pin and press to hold in place.

YOU WILL NEED

16 x 4½-in. (11-cm) squares of assorted cotton print fabrics

White cotton/linen fabric

Piece 1: 23¼ x 23¼ in. (59 x 59 cm) for the front
Piece 2: 23¼ x 12½ in. (59 x 32 cm) for the back
Piece 3: 23¼ x 15¾ in. (59 x 40 cm) for the back

Approx 96 in. (2.5 m) white bobble edging
3 buttons, 1 in. (2.5 cm) in diameter

22-in. (56-cm) square pillow form (cushion pad)

finished size:

22 in. (56 cm) square

4 Center the patchwork panel right side up on piece 1 (the pillow front), pin it in place, and press. Using a zig-zag stitch, machine stitch the patchwork to the pillow front. Stitch along the seams of the patchwork, starting along the central lines and working out, and finally zig-zag around all four edges.

5 Fold one long edge of piece 2 under by 2 in. (5 cm). Pin and press. Remove the pins and open out the fold. Fold the raw edge in to meet the press mark, then fold along the press line again and make a 1-in. (2.5-cm) hem. Pin, press, and machine stitch close to the edge. Repeat along one long edge of piece 3.

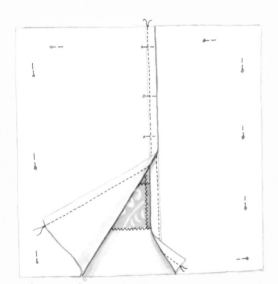

6 Place the patchwork front panel right side up on your work surface, with the smaller back piece right side down on top, the hemmed edge facing inward. Lay the larger back piece right side down on the opposite edge of the front panel, again with the hemmed edge facing inward, overlapping the smaller piece. Pin in place.

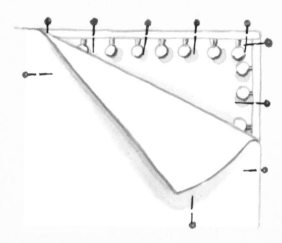

7 Sandwich the bobble trim between the front and back pieces around all four sides, with the bobbles facing inward. Pin in place.

8 Machine stitch all around the edge, using a ⅝-in. (1.5-cm) seam. Trim the corners diagonally. Turn the cover right side out.

9 Mark three evenly spaced buttonholes (see page 130) along the hemmed edge of the shorter (top) back piece and make buttonholes using your machine.

10 Hand stitch the buttons in place on the larger back piece. Insert the pillow form (cushion pad).

yo-yo pillow

This is a simple and pretty pillow, made using appliquéd yo-yos. Use a neutral background for the front, as you won't see it under the yo-yos, and a pretty contrasting fabric for the back to match the colors of the yo-yo fabrics; here we used toile de jouy.

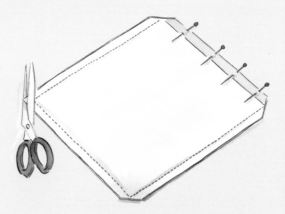

YOU WILL NEED

19¼ x 19¼ in. (49 x 49 cm) green toile de jouy for the back of the pillow

19¼ x 19¼ in. (49 x 49 cm) mediumweight cotton fabric for the front of the pillow

Approx. 95 x 6½-in. (16-cm) circles of assorted fabrics for the yo-yos

18 x 18-in. (46 x 46-cm) pillow form (cushion pad)

finished size:

18 x 18 in. (46 x 46 cm)

1 Pin the toile de jouy and mediumweight cotton pieces right sides together around the side and bottom edges. Turn the top edges over by ⅝ in. (1.5 cm), press, and pin. Machine stitch around the side and bottom edges, using a ⅝-in. (1.5-cm) seam. Remove the pins from the side and bottom edges and trim all four corners diagonally. Press the seams open and turn right side out.

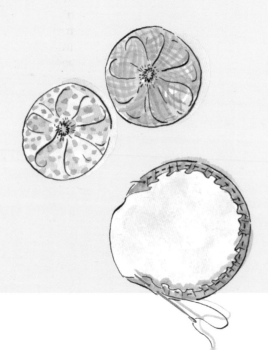

2 Make the yo-yos, following the instructions on page 131.

3 Hand stitch yo-yos onto the cotton side of the cover, placing them close together.

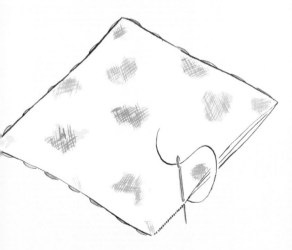

4 Insert the pillow form (cushion pad). Whip stitch (see page 138) the top edge of the cover to close.

Brighton belle pillow

Inspired by yachts off the seaside town of Brighton, on the south coast of England, this is so pretty and simple to make. It's a great way to use combine patchwork, appliqué and embroidery to make a stunning pillow for inside the home or in the garden.

YOU WILL NEED

Templates on page 142

Scraps of cotton fabric for the appliqué

Embroidery floss (thread) in colors of your choice

9½ x 9½-in. (24.5 x 24.5-cm) panel for the front

Four 13½ x 4-in. (34 x 10-cm) pieces of fabric for the side panels

15 x 17½-in. (38 x 44.5-cm) piece of fabric for back piece 1

11½ x 17½-in. (29 x 38-cm) piece of fabric for back piece 2

16 x 16-in. (40.5 x 40.5-cm) pillow form (cushion pad)

Three x 1 in. (2.5 cm) buttons

finished size:
16 x 16 in. (40.5 x 40.5 cm)

1 Trace the templates on page 142 onto fabric and cut out. Using the photo as a guide, following the instructions on page 132, appliqué and embroider the boat onto the front panel. The appliquéd sails are attached using a small machine zig-zag stitch, the ropes and outline of the boat are embroidered in backstitch, and the flag in satin stitch (see page 138).

2 With right sides together, pin the first side panel along the right-hand edge of the center panel; it will overhang at the bottom of the panel. Using a ¼-in. (6-mm) seam, stitch from ¼ in. (6 mm) down from the top edge to 1 in. (2.5 cm) above the bottom edge of the center piece. Press the seam to one side, toward the side panel.

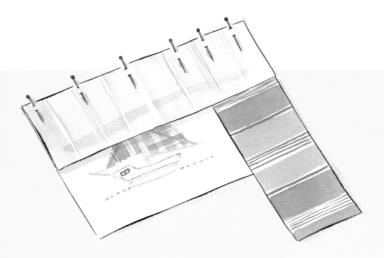

3 With right sides together, using a ¼-in. (6-mm) seam, pin and machine stitch the second side panel along the top edge of the center panel, continuing your stitching along the top edge of side panel 1. Press the seam to one side, toward the side panel.

4 With right sides together, starting at the top of side panel 2, pin the third side panel along the left-hand edge of the center panel. Machine stitch, using a ¼-in. (6-mm) seam. Press the seam toward the side panel.

5 With right sides together, starting at the bottom edge of side panel 3, pin side panel 4 along the bottom edge of the center panel. Using a ¼-in. (6-mm) seam, machine stitch, stopping about ¼ in. (6 mm) before the edge of side panel 1. Press the seam to one side, toward the side panel.

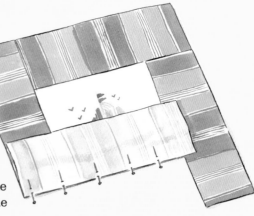

6 Place the piece on a flat surface and turn side panel 1 over so that the right side is facing the right side of the center piece. Starting at the end of the stitching on side panel 1, sew down to bottom edge of side panel 4, using a ¼-in. (6-mm) seam as before. Press the seam to one side.

7 Trim the whole front panel to 16½ in. (42 cm) square. Press well.

8 Fold over and press 2 in. (5 cm) to the wrong side along one long edge of back piece 1. Open out the fold, then fold the raw edge under to meet the pressed line. Fold over again to make a 1-in. (2.5-cm) double hem. Press, pin, and machine stitch. Repeat with back piece 2.

9 With right sides together, place back piece 1 on the front piece at the top. Place back piece 2 on top of piece 1, with the hemmed edges overlapping. Pin and machine stitch around all four sides, using a ⅝-in. (1.5-cm) seam. Trim each corner diagonally.

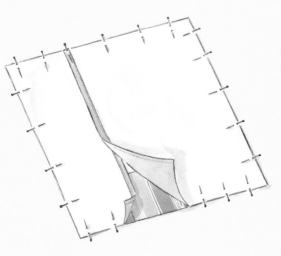

10 Make three buttonholes evenly spaced along the hemmed edge of back piece 1 (see page 130).

11 Turn the cover right side out. Sew buttons in place along the hemmed edge of back piece 2 to correspond with the buttonholes.

draft excluder

Keep the drafts at bay with this sweet draft excluder. Strips of fabric are joined together to form a long sausage shape, which is then filled with stuffing to help keep your home cozy and warm. Try to buy cotton stuffing rather than synthetic, as it is much weightier. If this is unavailable, put some dried beans or rice inside with the stuffing to make it heavier.

YOU WILL NEED

Scraps of fabric at least 15 in. (38 cm) long

45 in. (114 cm) bobble fringe

45 in. (114 cm) ribbon

Stuffing

finished size:
34 in. (85 cm) long

1 Cut strips of fabric in varying widths each 15 in. (38 cm) long. Move them around until you are happy with the arrangement. With right sides together and starting at one end, pin and stitch two of the strips together. Press the seam open.

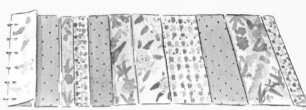

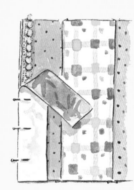

2 Continue to join the strips in this way, pressing the seams open as you go. To add the bobble fringe, lay a length of it along one raw edge of fabric on the right side and baste (tack) it in position. Lay the next strip into this with right sides together and machine stitch. The finished panel should be about 34 in. (85 cm) long, although you may wish to make a longer version for a wider door. Add more strips if you are making a longer one.

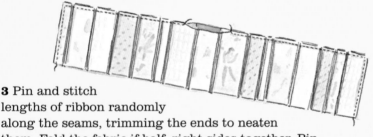

3 Pin and stitch lengths of ribbon randomly along the seams, trimming the ends to neaten them. Fold the fabric if half, right sides together. Pin and machine stitch along all three sides (not the folded side) leaving an opening of about 6 in. (15 cm). Trim the corners and turn right side out. Press.

4 Fill the cover with stuffing, pushing it into the corners and spreading it evenly inside. Hand stitch the opening closed.

kitchen & dining room

windmill table runner

Each "windmill" in this traditional patchwork design is made up of four pieces; twelve windmills are then put together to make the table runner. The beauty of the design lies in the combination of neutral shades and bright highlights.

level: experienced

YOU WILL NEED

Templates on page 140

Approx 10 x 10 in. (25 x 25 cm) cotton print fabric, or scraps of 9 different fabrics for the patchwork

19 x 50 in. (48 x 127 cm) cotton fabric for backing

19 x 50 in. (48 x 127 cm) batting (wadding)

1 yd (1 m) cotton print for binding

finished size:

15¾ x 45 in. (40 x 114.5 cm)

1 Enlarge the templates on page 140 by 200 percent. Cut one piece of fabric using Template A, one piece using Template B, and two pieces using Template C. Fold fabric pieces A and B in half at the point to mark the center points. Open the pieces out.

2 With right sides and raw edges together, matching the two center lines, pin the long edge of piece A to the short edge of piece B. Machine stitch, using a ¼-in. (6-mm) seam. Press the seam toward piece A.

3 Place one piece C on top of pieces A and B along one of the long edges, with right sides together, making sure there is an overhang where the three pieces join. Pin, machine stitch, and press the seam toward piece C.

4 Attach the remaining piece C to the other long edge of pieces A and B, with the same overhang. Pin in place, machine stitch, and press the seam toward piece C.

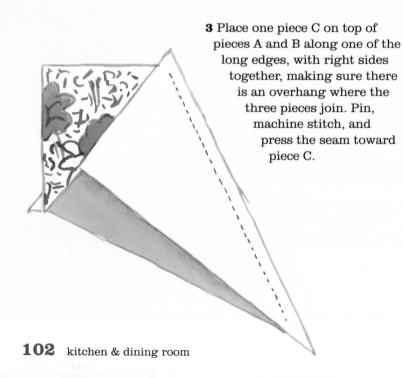

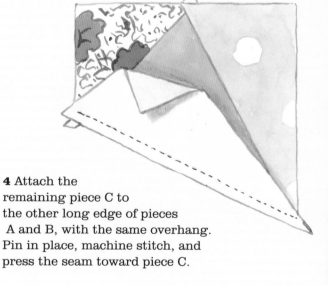

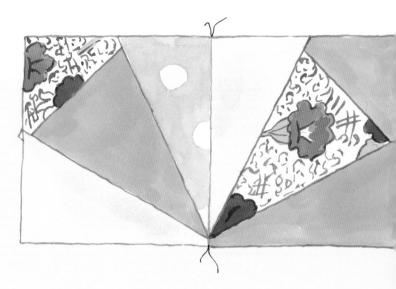

5 Repeat steps 1–4 three times more to make up the four units you need for a complete windmill block.

6 Place two units right sides together, aligning them along the edge of two C pieces. Pin and machine stitch, using a ¼-in. (6-mm) seam. Press the seam to one side. Repeat with the remaining two units, pressing the seam in the opposite direction.

7 Place the two pairs right sides together along the long edges of the C pieces, pin, and machine stitch, making sure that all the points meet at the center. Press the seams to one side.

stitch advice

If you press the seam on one pair of units to the left and the seam between the other two units to the right, this is called "nesting": it makes it easier to line up the points more accurately.

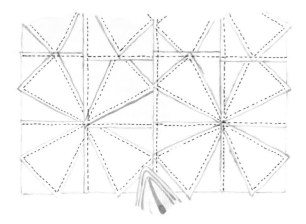

8 Repeat steps 1–7 eleven times, so that you have twelve windmills in total.

9 With right sides together, pin and machine stitch the windmills together in two strips of six, matching the seams. Press the seams to one side, in different directions in each row. Join the two strips together. Press the seam to one side.

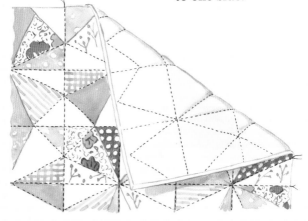

10 Assemble the three layers of the quilt "sandwich" (see page 133). Using curved safety pins and starting in the center of the table runner and working outward, pin through all layers to secure well, smoothing the table runner as you go. Quilt "in the ditch" (see page 134) along the center lines and two other seams.

11 Make a strip of bias binding approx. 132 x 2½ in. (3.3 m x 6 cm). Bind the table runner, following the instructions on page 138.

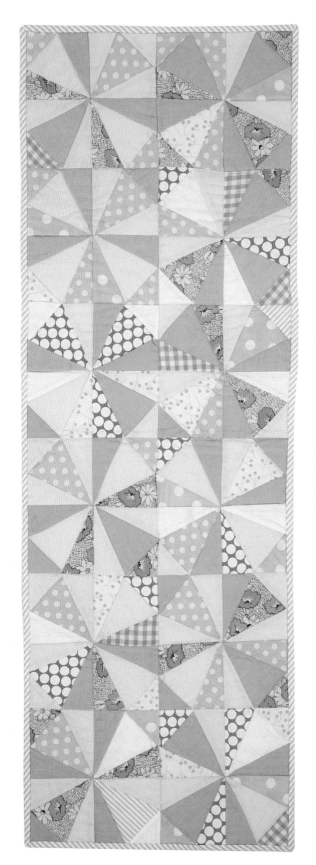

cake tea cozy

level: beginner/intermediate

YOU WILL NEED

Templates on page 142

Two 12 x 15-in. (30.5 x 38-cm) pieces of blue spotted fabric for the front and back

Two 12 x 15-in. (30.5 x 38-cm) pieces of pink floral print fabric for the lining

Four 12 x 15-in. (30.5 x 38-cm) pieces of thick batting (wadding)

6 x 6 in. (15 x 15 cm) white cotton fabric for the cake

11 scraps of different fabrics for the flowers

11 small circles of white cotton fabric for the flower centers

Fabric adhesive spray

Thick navy-blue thread (for freehand embroidery)

Pink embroidery floss (thread)

3 x 6 in. (8 x 15 cm) pink floral fabric for the tab

finished size:

13½ x 10½ in. (34.5 x 27 cm)

This is the prettiest thing to adorn your tea table you'll ever have—and it's so simple. It's a great way of learning to freehand machine embroider and quilt at the same time. Don't worry if your appliqué fabrics start to fray on the outside edges of the stitching, as this gives the flowers and cake a 3-D effect and makes the cake stand out really well.

1 Enlarge the templates on page 142 by 200 percent. Using the tea cozy template, cut two pieces of blue spotted fabric for the front and back and two pieces of pink floral fabric for the lining. Cut four pieces of batting (wadding) from same template, ½ in. (1 cm) shorter in length at the bottom edge. Cut one cake shape, 11 flowers, and 11 flower centers from the appropriate fabrics.

2 Spray the cake fabric on the wrong side with fabric adhesive and center it on the front of the tea cozy fabric. Place the fabric in an embroidery hoop if you wish. Freehand embroider around the outline of the cake, using navy-blue thread.

3 Spray adhesive onto the wrong side of two of the flowers and flower centers. Place each flower at the base edges of the cake and freehand embroider two lines around the outline of the flowers and centers.

4 Working in toward the center of the cake base, apply five more flowers and centers in the same way, overlapping them a little, so that you have seven flowers along the base in a slightly curved line.

stitch advice

When freehand embroidering, put the feed dogs in the down position before you start sewing and practice with and without an embroidery hoop to see which suits you best. Change the foot on your machine for a darning/embroidery foot.

Set the machine so that the needle is in the down position when it stops. This way you'll be able to keep your embroidery stable when taking a break from sewing or adjusting your fabric.

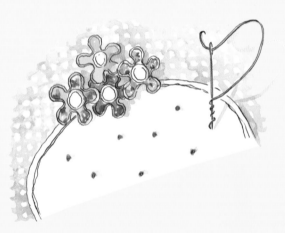

5 Apply three flowers to the top of the cake, with the last flower on top of the middle one, in the same way. Using pink embroidery floss (thread), work about 15 French knots (see page 138) evenly over the front of the cake. Remove the fabric from the embroidery hoop, if using, and press well.

6 Fold each long raw edge of the tab over to the wrong side by ½ in. (1 cm) and press. Fold the piece in half lengthwise, enclosing the raw edges, and press. Machine stitch along the long, unfolded edge, close to the edge.

7 Place two pieces of batting (wadding) on the wrong sides of the front and back pieces, aligning the top edges; the batting is ½ in. (1 cm) shorter than the front and back along the bottom edge. Pin well, using quilting pins.

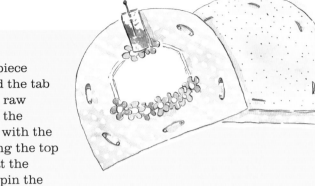

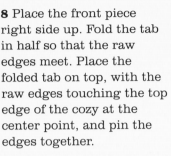

8 Place the front piece right side up. Fold the tab in half so that the raw edges meet. Place the folded tab on top, with the raw edges touching the top edge of the cozy at the center point, and pin the edges together.

9 Place the back of the cozy right side down on top, pin, and baste (tack) the front and back together. Remove the quilting pins. Using a walking foot, sew a 1-in. (2.5-cm) seam around the curved edge of the cozy, incorporating the tab.

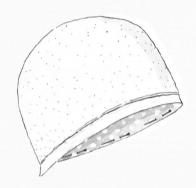

10 Trim the seam well, removing the bulk of the batting (wadding). Remove the basting (tacking) stitches. Turn the bottom edge of the main fabric up over the batting (wadding) and pin in place.

11 Pin the lining pieces right sides together. Machine stitch around the curved edge only, using a 1-in. (2.5-cm) seam. Trim the edges and press the seam open. Fold up the bottom edge by 1½ in. (4 cm) and press.

12 Turn the lining right side out and slip it over the top of the main piece, wrong sides together. Pin the lining along the bottom edge of the main piece, press and whip stitch in place (see page 138).

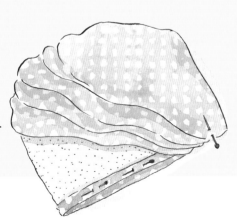

13 Make three or four small hand stitches at the top of the front and back of the cozy, stitching through all layers. Turn the cozy right side out.

chair seat covers

Far too nice to sit on, but if you're going to have a seat cover then these are the ones! They're a unique and charming way of decorating chairs for either inside the house or in the garden.

YOU WILL NEED

9½ x 18 in. (24 x 46 cm) floral print fabric and 9½ x 18 in. (24 x 46 cm) spotted print fabric for front cover

18 x 18 in. (46 x 46 cm) backing fabric for front cover

18 x 18 in. (46 x 46 cm) batting (wadding)

18 x 18 in. (46 x 46 cm) fabric for back cover

Template on page 142

Five x 5-in. (12.5-cm) squares, in five different patterned fabrics

One x 3-in. (7-cm) square of fabric for flower center

60 x 1¼ in. (1.5 m x 3 cm) fabric for ties

Embroidery floss (thread) to match flower

Spray starch

Freezer paper

finished size:
To fit pillow form (cushion pad) approx. 15 x 16 in. (38 x 41 cm)

Adjust size to your own requirements

1 Place the spotted and floral print fabrics for the front of the cover right sides together. Using a ¼-in. (6-mm), machine stitch the panels together along one long edge. Press the seam toward the darker fabric.

2 Place the backing fabric for the front cover right side down, with the batting (wadding) on top and the front panel right side up on top of the batting (wadding). Pin the three layers together. Taking the center seam line of the front cover as your point of reference, quilt lines 1 in. (2.5 cm) apart, running in the same direction as the seam. Trim the backing fabric and batting (wadding) level with the front cover.

3 Trace the petal template on page 142 onto card and cut out. Place the template on freezer paper, draw around it to make five paper petals, and cut out. Transfer the markings from the template to the paper petals.

stitch advice
When using freezer paper, always press on the matt side, not the shiny side.

4 Place the freezer-paper petals shiny side down on the wrong side of the fabric, and press. Draw a ¼-in. (6-mm) seam allowance around each freezer-paper petal on the back of the fabric.

5 Place two petals right sides together, aligning the markings. Using a ¼-in. (6-mm) seam, machine stitch from the center edge up to the marked point on one side. Press the seam to one side. Join two more petals in the same way.

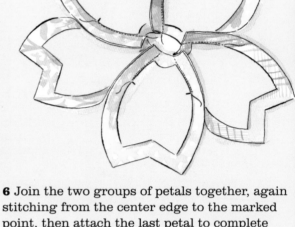

6 Join the two groups of petals together, again stitching from the center edge to the marked point, then attach the last petal to complete the flower. Press all the seams to one side, all in the same direction. At the center top of each petal, snip the fabric up to the edge of the freezer paper.

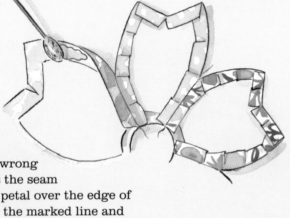

7 Spray a little starch into the lid of the can. Using a cotton bud and working on one petal at a time, paint the starch around the seam allowance on the wrong side of the fabric. Press the seam allowance around each petal over the edge of the freezer paper along the marked line and remove the freezer-paper templates.

8 Pin and baste (tack) the flower in position on the quilted front cover.

9 Trace the flower center template on page 142 onto template plastic or cardboard, and cut out. Place the template on the wrong side of the flower center fabric and draw around it, adding a ¼-in. (6-mm) seam allowance. Cut out. Work a line of running stitch along the center of the seam allowance, leaving the thread attached with a long tail. Place the template on the wrong side of the fabric and pull the threads up tight to gather the flower center. Spray a little starch on the inside of the flower center and lightly press. (If you are using a plastic template, take care not to melt it.)

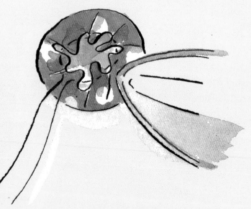

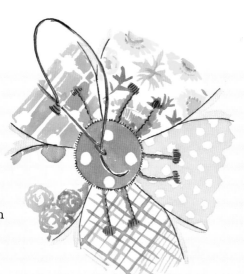

10 Pin and baste (tack) the flower center onto the flower. Hand stitch the flower in place, using tiny whip stitches (see page 138), then whip stitch around the flower center. Using two strands of embroidery floss (thread), embroider stamens using a combination of backstitch and satin stitch (see page 138).

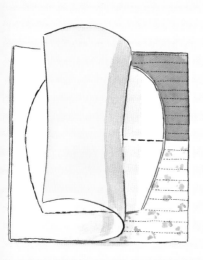

11 Place the pillow front right side up on a flat surface. Mark the center of the pillow form (cushion pad) from side to side. Align the center line of the pillow form (cushion pad) with the seam of the front, and place the pillow form (cushion pad) on top. Place the backing fabric right side down on top. Draw around the outline of the pillow form (cushion pad) on the backing fabric, then remove the pillow form (cushion pad).

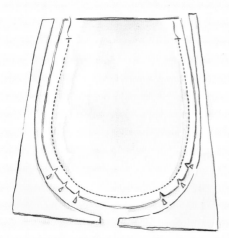

12 Pin the backing fabric to the pillow front, right sides together. Make a mark on each side of the backing fabric, ⅝ in. (1.5 cm) down from the top edge. Machine stitch the front to the backing fabric along the outline that you drew in the previous step, starting and finishing at the marked points.

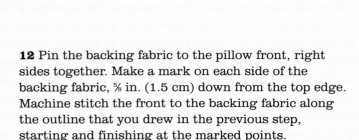

13 Trim the cover ¼ in. (6 mm) beyond the stitching line, leaving the top (straight) edge untrimmed. Cut two or three snips into the curved edges, taking care not to cut through the stitching. Press the seams open.

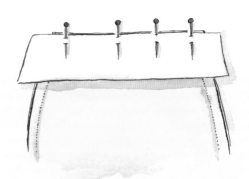

14 Measure the width of the unstitched edge of the cover and cut a strip of backing fabric to this measurement plus 1¼ in. (3 cm) by 3 in. (7 cm). Turn the cover right side out. With right sides together, center the strip on the top edge of the backing fabric, pin it in place and, using a ⅝-in. (1.5-cm) seam, machine stitch it in place.

15 Fold in the overhanging edges on each side of the flap, turn the flap over, and tuck it inside the cover. Turn the cover wrong side out.

16 Cut a strip of backing fabric, as in step 11. With right sides together, center the strip on the top edge of the front of the cover, pin it in place and, using a ⅝-in. (1.5-cm) seam, machine stitch. Fold in the overhanging edges on each side of the flap, turn the flap over, and tuck it inside the cover. Turn the cover wrong side out. Fold the top (raw) edge of the flap to the stitching line, then fold it once more. Pin and hand sew along all the edges of the fold, using whipping stitches (see page 138). Turn the cover right side out.

17 Cut a fabric strip measuring 60 x 1¼ in. (1.5 m x 3 cm). Press it in half lengthwise, open the strip out flat, and press the long raw edges over to the wrong side to meet at the central press line. Refold the strip with the raw edges inside. Pin, press, and machine stitch the long pressed edges together.

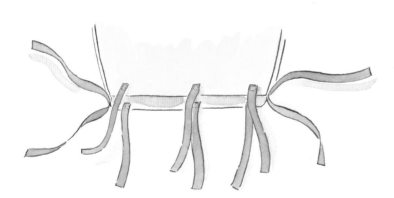

18 Cut two 17½-in. (45-cm) and six 4-in. (10-cm) pieces from the tie. Fold in the raw edges and hand stitch one of the longer ties on each side and three small ties evenly spaced along the top flap. Attach three small ties 2½ in. (6 cm) down from the top edge of the backing to correspond with the flap ties.

vintage kitchen tablecloth

It's very refreshing when you can create a new design from something that has been sitting in the cupboard for years. Many of the dish towels used here are ones that I've collected on my travels and it gives the whole family great pleasure to hear the stories linked to them. Everyone has his or her own favorite piece.

1 Press all the dish towels well to remove any creases. Lay them out in your chosen order on a large, flat surface. Horizontal designs go well at each end of the table, facing outward, so you can read and view the pictures as you eat.

> **level:** beginner

YOU WILL NEED

Vintage dish towels

Backing fabric

Jumbo rick-rack to fit around all four sides

Sizing

To work out how big you need to make your tablecloth, measure your table and add 10 in. (25 cm) on each side for the overhang. It's best to use more dish towels than you need, as you can always trim them to size later.

2 With right sides together, using a ⅝-in. (1.5-cm) seam, pin and machine stitch the dish towels together in strips. Trim the seam allowances and cut off any thick hems. Press the seams to one side.

3 Pin and machine stitch the strips together, again with a ⅝-in. (1.5-cm) seam. Trim around the edges so that all edges are straight.

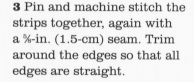

4 Cut a piece of backing fabric 1 in. (2.5 cm) bigger all around than the pieced tablecloth top. If your lining fabric is not wide enough, join two lengths together to achieve the size required.

5 Fold under the edges on all four sides of the tablecloth by ½ in. (1 cm) and pin.

6 Lay the backing fabric right side down on a flat surface and smooth out any creases. Center the tablecloth right side up on top. Smooth out all creases and pin the layers together with quilting pins.

7 Sew along each seam of the tablecloth using a straight stitch, stopping 1 in. (2.5 cm) from the edges. This will secure the backing fabric to the main piece and leave you space to turn the hems under at the edges.

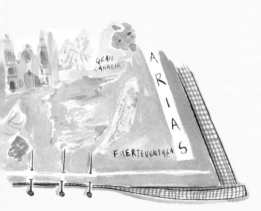

8 Lay the tablecloth on a flat surface and fold under the raw edges of the backing to match the folded-under edges of the tablecloth. Pin together and machine stitch close the edge. Press the edges.

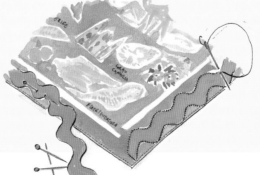

9 Pin jumbo rick-rack around the outside edges and whip stitch it in place along both edges (see page 138).

Dresden Plate place mats

The Dresden Plate is a popular patchwork design. I particularly like it, because you can play with all sorts of fabric combinations. Its height of popularity was in the 1920s and '30s, when feedsacks were often used. It works really well as a place mat: make one for each member of the family.

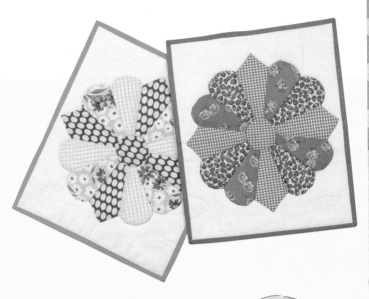

YOU WILL NEED

For each place mat

Templates on page 140

10 x 10 in. (26 x 26 cm) each of three different fabrics for the Dresden Plate design

15 x 13 in. (38 x 31 cm) white cotton fabric for the background fabric

15 x 13 in. (38 x 31 cm) white cotton fabric for backing

15 x 13 in. (38 x 31 cm) batting (wadding)

55 in. (140 cm) bias binding, 1 in. (2.5 cm) wide

Spray starch

finished size:

13 x 11 in. (33 x 28 cm)

1 Trace the templates on page 140 onto template plastic or cardstock and cut out. Using fabrics of your choice, cut out four pointed and eight rounded petals. Transfer all markings to the wrong side of the fabric pieces.

2 Join two rounded petals wrong sides together along one long edge, using a ¼-in. (6-mm) seam, stitching from the narrow edge to the marker point.

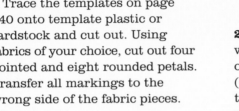

3 Continue to join pieces together in this way, placing one pointed petal piece in between each two rounded pieces. When the "flower" is complete, press all the seams to one side, all in the same direction. Using a small pair of sharp scissors, make a few small snips around the rounded edges of the petals, taking care not to cut into the stitching.

4 Spray a little starch into the lid of the container. Using a cotton bud, paint starch around the ¼-in. (6-mm) seam allowance of the petal tips. Fold under and press the seam allowance around the petal tips in by ¼ in. (6 mm).

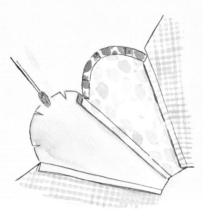

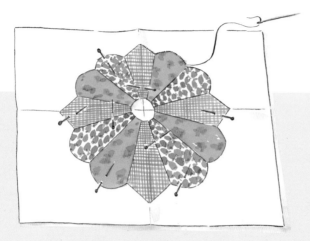

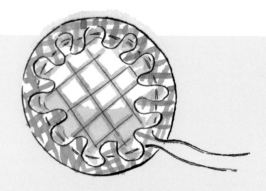

5 Fold the background fabric into quarters to mark the center. Open out and place the Dresden Plate in the center, aligning the pointed petal tips with the creased lines. Pin in place. Hand stitch the Dresden Plate to the background fabric, using tiny whip stitches (see page 138).

6 Using the template, cut out the flower center. Fold under the seam allowance by ¼ in. (6 mm) and work a line of running stitch all around. Pull up the threads to gather the flower center and press. Remove the template.

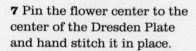

7 Pin the flower center to the center of the Dresden Plate and hand stitch it in place.

8 Place the backing fabric right side down on a flat surface with the batting (wadding) on top and the Dresden Plate right side up on top of the batting (wadding). Pin well. Quilt "in the ditch" (see page 134) along the seam of each petal and around the flower center.

9 Machine quilt a flower in the corners of the place mat.

10 Trim the place mat to 13 x 11 in. (33 x 28 cm). Bind the edges with ready-made bias binding (see page 138).

quilted trivets

These trivets are a great quilting project for beginners. They are just like mini quilts and are a good exercise in choosing colors, cutting accurately, and matching corners. Arrange the squares into a design of your choice, either randomly or symmetrically. It's a great way of using up scraps, too.

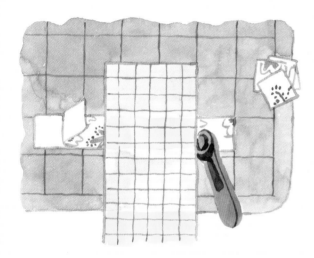

1 Using a rotary cutter and rule on a cutting mat (see page 128), cut your chosen fabrics into strips 2 in. (5 cm) wide, then cut the strips into squares. This is a good opportunity to practice cutting more than one strip at a time by stacking the strips. Arrange the squares in five rows of five.

2 With right sides together, using a ¼-in. (5-mm) seam, join the squares together in rows. Press the seams in each row to one side, all in the same direction.

YOU WILL NEED

25 x 2-in. (5-cm) squares for patchwork in assorted fabrics

8 x 8 in. (20 x 20 cm) backing fabric

8 x 8 in. (20 x 20 cm) batting (wadding)

2½ x 5½ in. (6.5 x 14 cm) fabric for tab

28 in. (71 cm) bias binding, 1½ in. (4 cm) wide

finished size:

8 x 8 in. (20 x 20 cm)

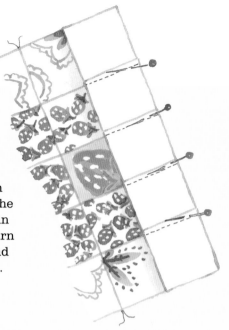

3 Join the rows together, taking care to align the seams of each row with those in the row above. Press the seams to one side, all in the same direction. Turn the patchwork over and press it from the front.

4 Cut the backing fabric to the same size as the patchwork, plus 1 in. (2.5 cm) all around. Cut a piece of batting (wadding) the same size as the backing fabric.

5 Lay the backing fabric right side down, with the batting (wadding) on top, and the patchwork right side up on top of the batting. Pin in several places to secure the three layers together.

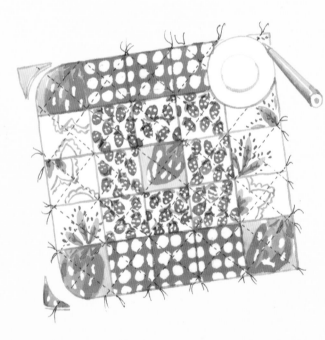

6 Starting at one corner, machine stitch a diagonal line from one corner to the other. Continue to sew diagonal lines across each square in both directions, using the illustration as a guide. Place a small, round object such as the lid of a box of pins on each corner in turn, draw around it, and round off the corners. Trim the backing fabric and batting (wadding) level with the patchwork if necessary.

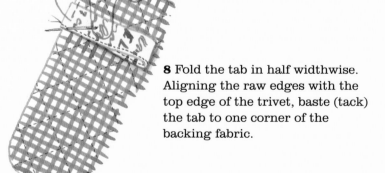

7 Fold the fabric for the tab in half lengthwise, press, then open out. Fold each raw edge in toward the center crease by ¼ in. (6 mm) and press. Fold the fabric along the center crease line again, and machine stitch along the edge.

8 Fold the tab in half widthwise. Aligning the raw edges with the top edge of the trivet, baste (tack) the tab to one corner of the backing fabric.

9 Open out the bias binding and pin it around the edge of the front of the trivet. Stitch it in place, following the instructions on page 138.

10 Flip the tab up so that the folded edge points outward and whipstitch the side edges to the binding, making sure your stitching only goes through the binding on the back of the trivet.

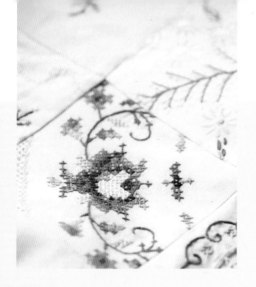

patchwork apron

I was very kindly given a bag full of old embroidered table cloths that had all been damaged and was inspired to recycle what was left of them into something beautiful. This apron is supposed to be functional, but it's so special you won't want to get it dirty; do your cooking in an old apron and pop this one on just before your guests arrive!

YOU WILL NEED

12 x 4¼-in. (11-cm) squares of embroidered fabric

21 x 17 in. (54 x 43 cm) white cotton fabric

27½ x 24 in. (70 x 61 cm) cotton print fabric

64 in. (163 cm) rick-rack, dark blue

27 in. (69 cm) decorative trim, 1 in. (2.5 cm) wide

finished size:

26 x 21 in. (66 x 53 cm)

1 Lay the squares of embroidered fabric out on a flat surface and arrange them in three rows of four. Mark the rows and the order of the squares (see page 130).

2 Sew the horizontal rows together first, using a ¼-in. (6-mm) seam and making sure you keep the squares in order. Press all the seams in each row to one side, all in the same direction.

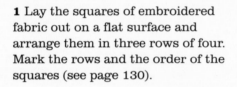

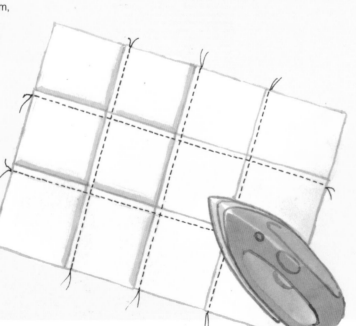

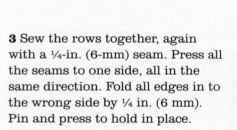

3 Sew the rows together, again with a ¼-in. (6-mm) seam. Press all the seams to one side, all in the same direction. Fold all edges in to the wrong side by ¼ in. (6 mm). Pin and press to hold in place.

4 Make a 2-in. (5-cm) double hem at the top and bottom of the main piece and a ¾-in. (2-cm) double hem on each side.

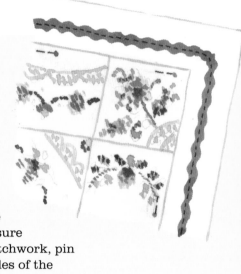

5 Center the patchwork piece on the white panel and pin it in place. Measure ¾ in. (2 cm) from the edge of the patchwork, pin rick-rack in place around all four sides of the patchwork, and machine stitch.

6 Press under ¾ in. (2 cm) to the wrong side on all sides of the white cotton panel and pin. Center the whole panel on the cotton print fabric and pin it in place. Using a straight stitch and white thread, machine stitch along each seam of the patchwork, sewing through all three layers. Remove the pins and press well.

7 Pin around the edges of the patchwork to hold it in place and, using contrasting thread, machine zig-zag stitch around all four sides of the patchwork. Press well.

8 Using a straight stitch and white thread, machine stitch around the edges of the white cotton panel. Press well.

9 Turn in each end of the decorative trim by about ½ in. (1 cm), pin to the bottom of the apron on the right side, and machine stitch in place.

10 Turn under the raw edges at each short end of the tie and press. Press under ¼ in. (1 cm) to the wrong side along each long edge. Fold the tie in half widthways so that the folded edges meet. Pin and machine stitch along the folded edge. Repeat to make the second tie.

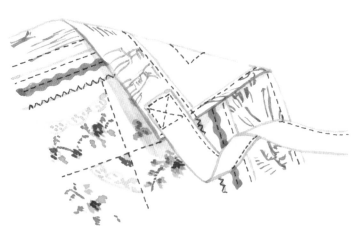

11 Pin one tie to each inside top edge of the apron, with the end of the tie 1½ in. (4 cm) from the side edge. Machine stitch across the short end of the tie, along for about 1 in. (2.5 cm), across the width of the tie again, and back to the starting point, forming a square of stitching. Sew diagonally across the square in both directions to reinforce the stitching.

general techniques

preparing fabrics

Patchwork began as a way of saving money by re-cycling dress fabrics into bed linen and, although patchwork fabrics are now manufactured specially for the purpose, the tradition of recycling continues to this day. If you're a vintage fabric magpie, think carefully before rushing into buying and check that the fabric hasn't perished or rotted. Pick up vintage or retro fabrics from thrift stores, markets, yard sales, and online sources such as ebay.

If you're not sure whether the color is going to run on your fabric, wet a small section of it and lay it on a white piece of toweling or kitchen paper; if it bleeds, you'll know it's not color fast. Don't use it or it will ruin the rest of your quilt.

Most cotton quilting fabrics don't shrink, but you may prefer to wash the fabrics first. There is no need to wash batting (wadding) before use.

If you intend to give your quilt as a gift or to sell it, try washing the quilt when it's completely finished, so that if anything is going to happen you can rectify it.

Always press fabrics before you use them. You can use a steam iron if you prefer and this helps if the fabrics are particularly creased.

stitch advice
Old fabrics that have been washed a lot lose their crispness. Use spray starch on fabrics to crisp them up and give them some life.

using a rotary cutter and mat

A rotary cutter allows you to cut very accurately and saves time if you have lots of patchwork pieces to cut, as you can cut through several layers at the same time. Only use a rotary cutter with a proper quilting ruler made from Perspex. These are thick enough to the keep the cutter from slipping and cutting your fingers. They come in a wide range of sizes: I use one that measures 6½ x 24 in. (16.5 x 60 cm).

A self-healing mat provides an ideal surface for cutting. Most of the mats and rulers have grids and measurements in both imperial and metric.

Cut with the blade against the side of the ruler, using the weight of your arm to press down on the rotary cutter to give a clean cut.

Put your other hand and weight firmly down on the ruler to keep it still and in position. Don't let the ruler hang off the edge of the table. Always cut away from you, not toward you.

Take great care when using a rotary cutter: it is a very sharp tool and you should always retract the blade when you're not using it.

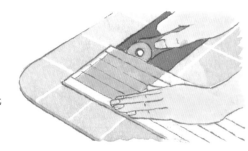

fussy cutting

Fussy cutting simply means cutting out a specific motif or section from the piece of fabric you want to use. Examples can be found in the Retro Crib Quilt (page 20) and the Patchwork Apron (page 124)

Either use a clear Perspex template and draw around the chosen area or measure and mark the fabric and cut with a rotary cutter or scissors.

working with templates

To make a template for a fabric shape, enlarge or reduce it on a photocopier to the required size. Simply cut out the shape with paper scissors and pin it to the fabric to use as a pattern piece. You can also make templates from parcel paper, freezer paper, cardboard and template plastic. Don't forget to copy any essential markings from the original template to your own.

cutting corners

Cut diagonally across the seam allowance at corners to eliminate bulk and to achieve neat right angles when the piece is turned right side out.

snipping curved edges

On curved seams, snip into the seam allowance to maintain smooth curves when the piece is turned right side out and the seam allowances are pressed flat.

inserting a centered zipper

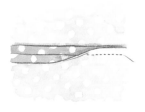
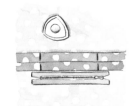
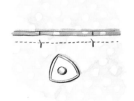
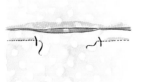
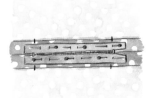

1 Pin the two main fabric pieces right sides together. Fold the top edge of each piece of fabric over to the wrong side by ⅝ in. (1.5 cm) and press. Lift up the folded-over edges and baste (tack) along the pressed line.

2 Remove the pins and press the basted seam open. Center the zipper on the seam, putting a chalk mark or a pin marker on the fabric at each end of the zipper teeth.

3 Remove the zipper and make another mark in the same place on the underside of the folded-over edges.

4 Place the two main pieces right sides together and machine stitch along the top edge to approx. ¼ in. (6 mm) beyond the first zipper marker. Take the fabric out of the machine and repeat on other side. Remove the pins and press the seam open.

5 Place the closed zipper wrong side down between the marked points, pin, and baste (tack) in place. Using a zipper foot if you have one, machine stitch the zipper in place. Remove all pins and basting (tacking) stitches. Open the zipper.

making buttonholes

Most sewing machines have a buttonhole foot. Following the manufacturer's instructions for your particular machine, set your machine to the size of your button and test it out on a scrap of fabric first.

1 Mark the placement of the required buttonhole on the fabric with tailor's chalk or similar.

2 Set your sewing machine to the buttonhole setting and follow the instructions.

3 Using a seam ripper or small, sharp scissors, cut a slit between the lines of zigzag stitches. Take care to not let your hand slip or to use too much pressure with the seam ripper or you will rip through the stitches.

patchwork

labeling patchwork pieces

After cutting out your fabric squares and laying out the design, it's essential to label the rows in the correct order. Either use sticky labels or pin a piece of paper labeled with the row number to the first square in each row; you may also find it helpful to mark whether this square is on the left or the right of the row, as it's very easy to make a mistake and start sewing the wrong way. Make a pile of all the squares in each row in the correct order and take each pile to the sewing machine in turn.

pressing patchwork

Keep the ironing board and iron close to where you're sewing.

In patchwork and quilting, seams are usually pressed to one side rather than open, but the project instructions will tell you exactly what to do. They are pressed open when you need the seams to be flat to reduce bulk—for example, on bag or cushion seams.

After you have made your quilt or patchwork top and pressed the seams from the wrong side, turn the work over and press it on the right side to set the seams. Use a "lower and lift" method to press, rather than dragging the iron back and forth across the fabric as you do when ironing a shirt. Be extra vigilant when pressing small pieces on the bias or strip piecing to avoid pressing them out of shape.

If you're using light and dark colors, press the seam toward the darker color to avoid the dark fabric showing through on the lighter fabric.

"nesting"

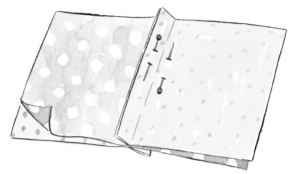

"Nesting" is a way of joining units or blocks to ensure the points meet accurately. This is achieved by pressing adjacent seams in opposite directions. Put the pieces to be joined right sides together, aligning the seams. Place a pin along the seam line to hold the pieces in place while sewing.

making yo-yos

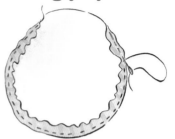
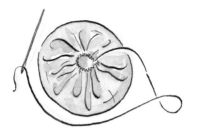

1 Cut circles of fabric to the size stated in the project instructions. Turn the edge of each fabric circle to the wrong side by about ¼ in. (6 mm). Using a needle and thread, work a line of small running stitches around the edge of the circle.

2 Gather up the stitches to close the center of the yo-yo. Push the needle right through the gathers to the other side in several directions around to secure the gathers. Tie and trim the thread to secure.

freestyle machine embroidery

Freestyle embroidery is very liberating and creative. It can be a bit scary when you're first starting out, but it really pays off with a bit of practice. It's a way of drawing using a needle and thread: treat the needle as you would a pencil.

You will have a lot more freedom when freestyle embroidering as the feed dogs are dropped allowing you to get your fingers closer to the needle as you guide the fabric around; take great care not to let your fingers get too close to avoid being pierced by the needle.

using a hoop

An embroidery hoop is necessary particularly if you are stitching onto one layer of fabric. If you are using a quilt sandwich, it's sometimes easier without a hoop. Always test a piece out first and see what works for you.

The hoop is made up of two circles of wood. Place the inner piece on a flat surface, then place the fabric on top, centering the area you want to embroider in the hoop. Place the outer circle on top, push down, and tighten the screw to keep the fabric sandwiched in between the two circles.

The hoop will keep the fabric taut and in position while you are sewing. Use a hoop the appropriate size for the motif and press the fabric well once you have removed the hoop.

dropping the feed dogs

Dropping the feed dogs will enable you to move your fabric around freely in any position. Refer to your own sewing machine manual for instructions on how to do this.

darning foot

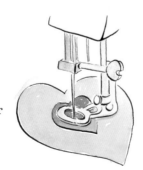

When freehand embroidering a darning foot is essential; most machine manufacturers supply these. Choose a Perspex one, if possible, so that you can see your stitches more easily.

appliqué

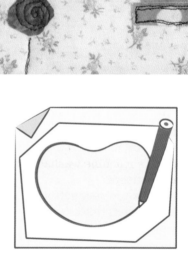

Appliqué means attaching a separate piece of fabric onto the main piece. This can be achieved by using hand or machine stitching. The appliqué piece is held in position with either fusible bonding web, pins, basting (tacking) stitches, or fabric spray adhesive.

There are several styles of stitching appliqué: you can use decorative machine zigzag stitches, blanket stitches (see page 139), or freestyle machine stitching just inside the outside edge of the appliqué, which creates a rough, frayed look.

method 1: fusible bonding web

1 Enlarge the template(s) to the required size (see page 129), trace onto thin card, and cut out. Cut a square of paper-backed fusible bonding web large enough to accommodate the appliqué motif. Lay the square on the wrong side of your appliqué fabric, adhesive side down, and press with a hot iron to heat bond.

2 Place the card template on the paper-backed side of the appliqué fabric and draw around it with a pencil. Carefully cut out the motif and peel away the paper backing.

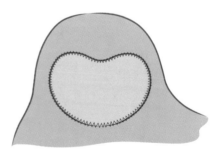

3 Place the motif, adhesive side down, on the main fabric and press with a hot iron to attach. For a professional finish, machine zig-zag stitch all around the motif.

method 2: fabric adhesive

1 Enlarge the template(s) to the required size (see page 129) and cut out. Pin the paper templates to your chosen fabrics and cut out. Remove the paper templates and pins and place the fabric motifs on your chosen background fabric. When you're happy with the arrangement, spray the back of the motifs lightly with fabric adhesive and re-position them on the background fabric.

2 Machine stitch around the edge of the motifs to fix them in position using a stitch of your choice.

assembling the quilt "sandwich"

This method is used for quilts that are going to have their edges bound (see page 135). The backing fabric needs to be about 2 in. (5 cm) larger than the quilt top all around. If your fabric isn't wide enough, cut two lengths and join them together in the center.

1 Press the backing fabric and cut it to the size of the quilt top plus at least 1 in. (2.5 cm) all around. (If the quilt is to be self-bound (see page 136), the backing fabric may need to be larger still; refer to the individual project instructions for the exact measurements.) Lay the backing fabric right side down on a flat surface, smooth it out, and tape it down to keep it in position.

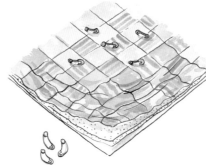

2 Cut a piece of batting (wadding) the same size as the backing fabric and lay it down on top. Lay the quilt top right side up on top of the batting (wadding), smoothing out all the creases.

3 Using curved safety pins or quilting pins and starting in the center of the quilt and working outward, pin through all layers to secure well, smoothing the quilt as you go. Use plenty of pins and take your time. Don't pin the seams if you intend to stitch "in the ditch" (see below).

batting (wadding)

Batting (wadding) is the soft padding in the center of a quilt. There are several varieties on the market.

Polyester is the cheapest, but it is slippery and more difficult to handle. It comes in a variety of thicknesses (loft) and your choice depends on how thick you want your quilt to look. It's machine washable, but doesn't breathe like the natural fibers.

Bamboo is very soft and ideal for people with allergies. It's easy to handle and generally needs to be hand washed, so always check the label for washing instructions. It tends to be more expensive than other fibers.

Wool is warm and must be hand washed. It's generally more expensive, warm, and nice to quilt with.

Cotton or cotton mixes are easy to source and best for a beginner as they don't shift around when quilting and can be machine washed.

Batting can be bought by the yard (metre) and off the roll, which is ideal as this way means there are no creases. It is also sold in cut-to-size bags, which are generally folded; you will need to lay or hang the batting to get the creases out and let it rest before using. It's available in a variety of widths, so work out your measurements carefully. On large quilts, you may need to join the wadding to ensure you have the correct width.

All battings have a recommended stitch distance. Unless you follow this guide, your batting may disintegrate within the quilt or move about.

quilting

Quilting simply means stitching the three layers together to hold them firmly in place.

When handling a large quilt such as the Log Cabin Quilt on page 10, it can be bulky and difficult to get into the machine. Roll your quilt on one side, with the rolled edge under the arm of the machine. Don't let the other side of the quilt drop onto the floor. It will be heavy and must be supported by a chair or over a sofa – whatever you have.

When quilting, always start sewing in the middle of the quilt and work outward. Stop after each seam to check there is no puckering.

When freehand quilting shapes, practice first. It may take a while to get the shape and the tension correct. If the machine is skipping stitches, this means the tension is either too loose or too tight. The secret is to practice on a small sample quilt sandwich before you start on your large quilt.

There are several different feet for quilting and it's worth having a look at the ones you can buy for your own machine. A walking foot with an open toe is a good investment, as is a ¼-in. (6-mm) quilting foot.

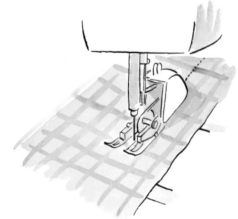

Walking foot

Quilting evenly spaced straight lines
Some machines have an arm that slots into the back of the walking foot, which you can set as a guide to quilting evenly spaced straight across your quilt. If you don't have one of these, you can mark up your fabric with a marking tool of your choice—tailor's chalk, invisible fabric pens, or masking tape.

Quilting "in the ditch"
Quilting "in the ditch" is done using a straight line of stitching along the seams between the patchwork pieces. Stitch very close to the seam, on the lower edge of the seam. Use a walking foot, which has feed dogs in the top and pushes the fabric from the top and the bottom and avoids the fabric slipping.

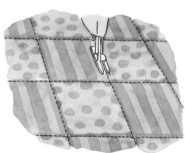

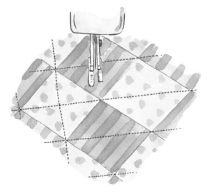

Diagonal quilting
Diagonal quilting consists of straight lines that run from one corner to the other and then from the opposite corner so that the stitching crosses the first line in the center.

Meander quilting
Use a walking foot and wiggly lines to create a wavy effect.

Quilting motifs
You can quilt motifs freehand by eye, or draw the motif on the fabric first using a fadeaway fabric marker pen. A darning foot is necessary for any freehand quilting.

It's more difficult to draw the motif on and machine around it. Freehand quilting takes a little confidence and perseverance, but it creates an original and artistic effect.

after quilting

Always trim the batting (wadding) with a straight edge after quilting—preferably with a rotary cutter and ruler, which will give a really defined edge ready for binding.

simple borders

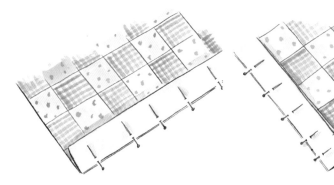

1 Cut two strips of fabric on the straight grain measuring the same as the top of the quilt by the required depth for the border. With right sides together, using a ¼-in. (6-mm) seam, pin and machine stitch the strips to the top and bottom of the quilt. Press the seams following the pattern instructions.

2 Measure the sides of the quilt, including the borders at the top and bottom, and cut two strips to this measurement by the required depth for the border. Attach these strips to the sides of the quilt, again using a ¼-in. (6-mm) seam. Press the seams following the pattern instructions and bind the edges of the quilt using your chosen method (see below).

binding

A binding is the edging of your quilt. It covers the raw edges of the quilt sandwich. A quilt may be either self bound (where the backing fabric is folded over to the front of the quilt—see page 140) or have a separate binding, which can be single- or double-fold (see page 140). For a large piece such as a quilt, a double-fold binding is stronger and protects the edges better. Bindings may be cut on the straight grain or on the bias; they can have straight or mitered corners.

self binding with straight corners

 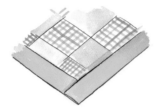  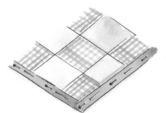 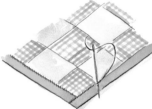

1 Trim the batting (wadding) to the same size as the quilt top, if necessary. On the wrong side of the backing fabric, mark a line 1 in. (2.5 cm) away from the quilt top, then cut the backing fabric along this line.

2 With quilt top facing upward, fold the backing fabric over the quilt top along one edge. Repeat on each side, making sure the folds are at right angles to the quilt top at the corners. Press the folds with your fingers.

3 Open out the folds of the backing fabric and fold the raw edges in so that they meet the raw edge of the quilt top.

4 Fold again so that the backing fabric overlaps the quilt top and pin in place.

5 Whip stitch the folded edge in place, using matching thread (see page 138).

single-fold binding with straight corners

  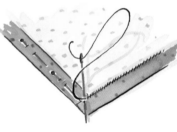

1 Cut binding strips the same length as each side of the quilt top plus approx. 1 in. (2.5 cm) and three times the desired depth of the finished binding plus ¼ in. (6 mm)—so if you want the binding to be ½ in. (12 mm) deep, cut it 1½ in. (3.6 cm) deep plus ¼ in. (6 mm).

2 With right sides together, aligning the raw edges, center the edge of the binding strip on the top edge of the quilt and pin in place. Machine stitch the binding in place, stitching the depth of the binding from the edge of the quilt— so if you want the binding to be ½ in. (12 mm) deep, stitch ½ in. (12 mm) from the edge. Repeat on the bottom edge of the quilt.

3 Turn the strips to the wrong side of the quilt top along the stitching line. Tuck the raw edge of the binding under by ¼ in. (6 mm) and pin or baste (tack) it in place. Tuck in the overlapping ends at the corners so that they are straight and the corners are at right angles.

4 Repeat steps 2 and 3 on each side of the quilt. At the corners, tuck the over-lapping fabric under so that it's level with the edge of the quilt and pin in place. Whip stitch all around the folded edges and tucked-under corners (see page 138).

Double-fold binding with straight corners

Cut binding strips the same length as each side of the quilt top plus 1 in. (2.5 cm) and six times the desired depth of the finished binding plus ¼ in. (6 mm)—so if you want the binding to be ½ in. (12 mm) deep, cut it 3 in. (7.5 cm) deep plus ¼ in. (6 mm). Fold the binding in half lengthwise and press. Attach the binding in the same way as for a single-fold binding, aligning the raw edges of the binding with the raw edges of the quilt.

Single-fold binding with mitered corners

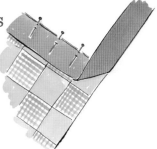
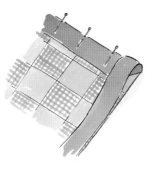

1 Cut strips three times the width you want the finished binding to be plus ½-in. (1-cm) seam allowances by the total perimeter of the quilt plus about 10 in. (25 cm) to allow for overlapping at the corners and when the two ends meet. Join the strips together to achieve the correct length if necessary.

2 With right sides together, aligning the raw edges, pin the binding along the edge of the quilt top. Starting in the middle of one long edge, machine stitch at your chosen distance from the quilt edge, leaving a tail of approx. 10 in. (25 cm). Lift the presser foot, take the quilt out of the machine, and place it on a flat surface. Fold the binding away from the quilt at an angle of 90°.

3 Refold the binding along the next edge of the quilt and pin it in place. Machine stitch from the very edge of the quilt of line you're about to sew. Continue around the other three edges in the same way, stopping a few inches (centimeters) from where you first started.

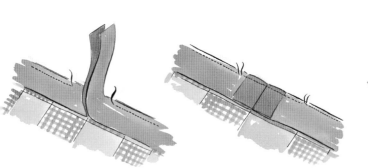

4 Match the two ends of the binding together and trim each end to approx. 2 in. (5 cm).

5 Pin the strips together close to the edge and sew along the pin line where the two fabrics meet. Trim the seam to approx. ¼ in. (6 mm). Press the seam open. Continue to stitch the binding to the main piece.

6 Fold the binding to the back of the quilt over the stitching line and tuck the raw edge under. Whip stitch in place, adding extra stitches to secure the mitered corners (see page 138).

Double-fold binding with mitered corners

For double-fold binding, cut strips six times the width you want the finished binding to be plus ½-in. (1-cm) seam allowances by the total perimeter of the quilt plus about 10 in. (25 cm) to allow for overlapping at the corners and when the two ends meet. Join the strips together to achieve the correct length if necessary. With wrong sides together, fold the binding in half lengthwise and press. Apply in the same way as for single-fold binding.

making bias binding

Bias binding is a piece of edging fabric that is cut on the bias of the fabric (diagonally against the grain). This gives the fabric more stretchiness and is often used for easing around curves.

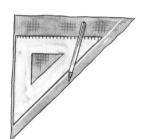

1 Using a set square and chalk, mark lines about 1½ in. (4 cm) apart at a 45° angle across the fabric Cut along the drawn lines.

2 To join strips together, place two pieces at right angles, draw a line from corner to corner, and pin either side. Sew along the line.

3 Trim approx. ¼ in. (6 mm) from the seam allowance and press the seam open. Continue to join the strips together until the bias strip is the required size for your project.

4 With wrong sides facing, press the strip in half along its length. Open the strip out flat and press the long, raw edges over to the wrong side to meet at the central fold line.

attaching bias binding

1 Open out the bias binding. With right sides together, aligning the raw edges, pin the binding to the edge that is being bound. Machine stitch along the first crease.

2 Fold the binding over along the stitching line to the wrong side of the piece, fold it under along the second crease line, pin, and then whip stitch in place.

stitches

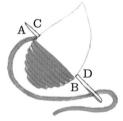

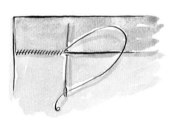

French knot
Bring the needle up from the back of the fabric to the front. Wrap the floss (thread) two or three times around the tip of the needle, then reinsert the needle at the point where it first emerged. The wraps will form a knot on the surface of the work.

Backstitch
Work from right to left. Bring the needle up one stitch length to the left of the end of the stitching line. Insert it one stitch length to the right and bring it up again one stitch length in front of the point from which it first emerged. Pull the thread through.

Satin stitch
This is a "filling" stitch that is used for motifs such as flower petals. Work from left to right. Draw the shape on the fabric, then work straight stitches across it, coming up at A and down at B, then up at C and down at D, and so on. Place the stitches next to each other so that no fabric is visible between them.

Whip stitch
This is used to sew to layers together along their edges. Start the stitch between the two layers and bring the needle through the front. At a slight diagonal angle, sew a stitch that overlaps the edge, passing the needle through the back fabric, and sewing through the two layers at another slight angle through to the front, just up from where you started.

Detached chain stitch
Work a single chain, as above, but fasten it by taking a small vertical stitch across the bottom of the loop.

templates

Blanket stitch
Starting between two layers of fabric, bring the needle up through the front. Sew a stitch that overlaps the edge at a right angle, passing the needle through the back fabric, sewing through both layers and coming out where it started. Leave a small loop and pass the needle through it from the front to the back and pull tight. Start the second stitch at the back, passing through both layers, emerging a small distance along the edge from the first stitch. Leave a small loop, pass the needle through it from front to back pull tight. Repeat along the whole edge.

Buggy Blanket, page 17

Enlarge all by 200%

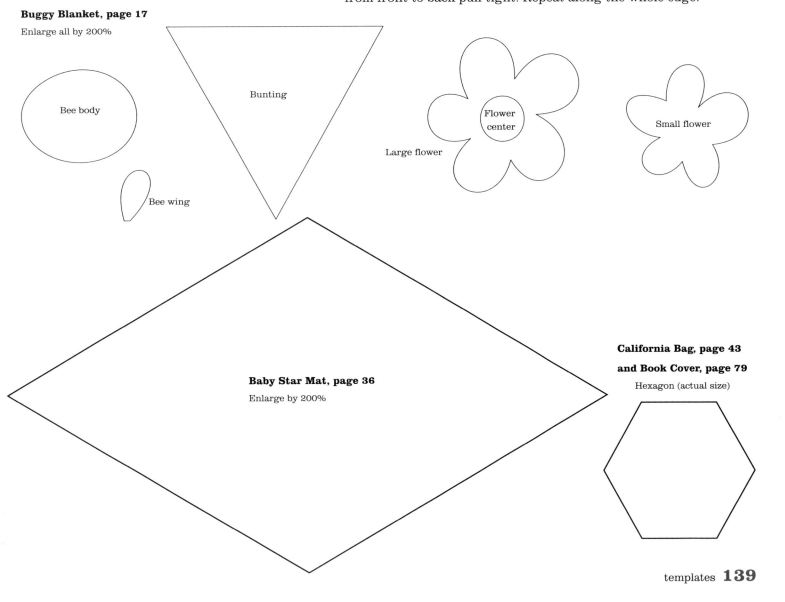

Bee body

Bee wing

Bunting

Large flower

Flower center

Small flower

Baby Star Mat, page 36

Enlarge by 200%

California Bag, page 43

and Book Cover, page 79

Hexagon (actual size)

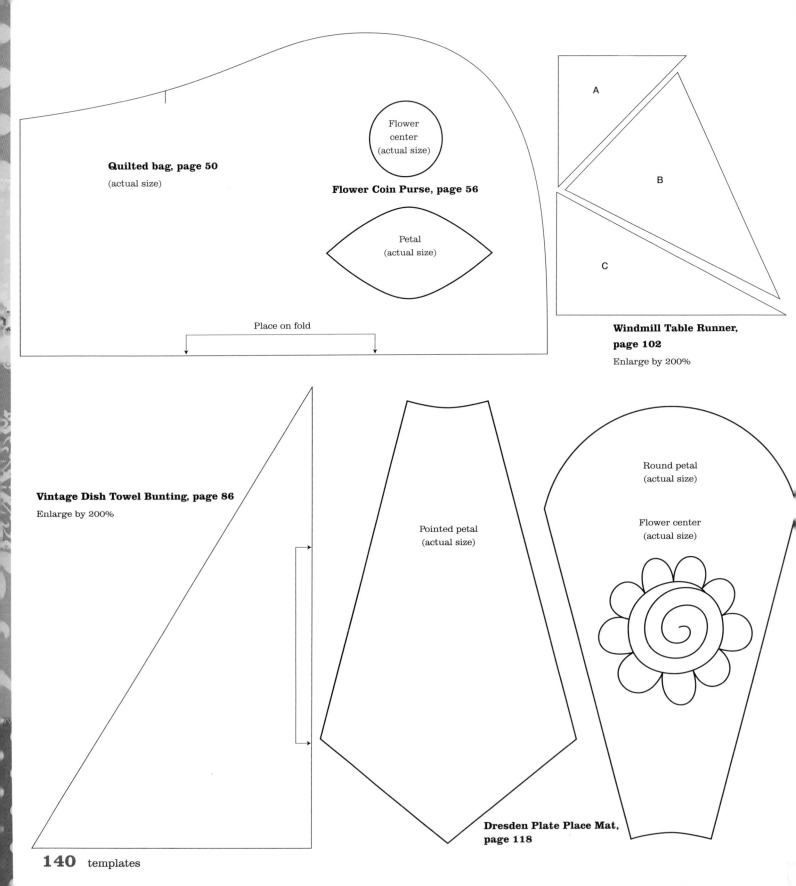

Quilted bag, page 50

(actual size)

Flower center
(actual size)

Flower Coin Purse, page 56

Petal
(actual size)

Place on fold

A

B

C

**Windmill Table Runner,
page 102**

Enlarge by 200%

Vintage Dish Towel Bunting, page 86

Enlarge by 200%

Pointed petal
(actual size)

Round petal
(actual size)

Flower center
(actual size)

**Dresden Plate Place Mat,
page 118**

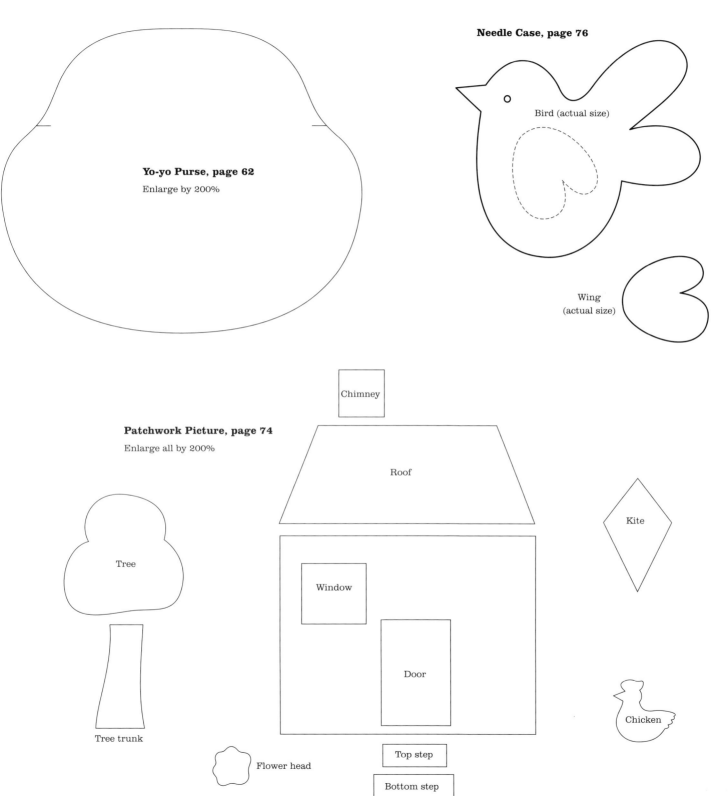

Needle Case, page 76

Bird (actual size)

Wing
(actual size)

Yo-yo Purse, page 62

Enlarge by 200%

Chimney

Patchwork Picture, page 74

Enlarge all by 200%

Roof

Kite

Tree

Window

Door

Chicken

Tree trunk

Flower head

Top step

Bottom step

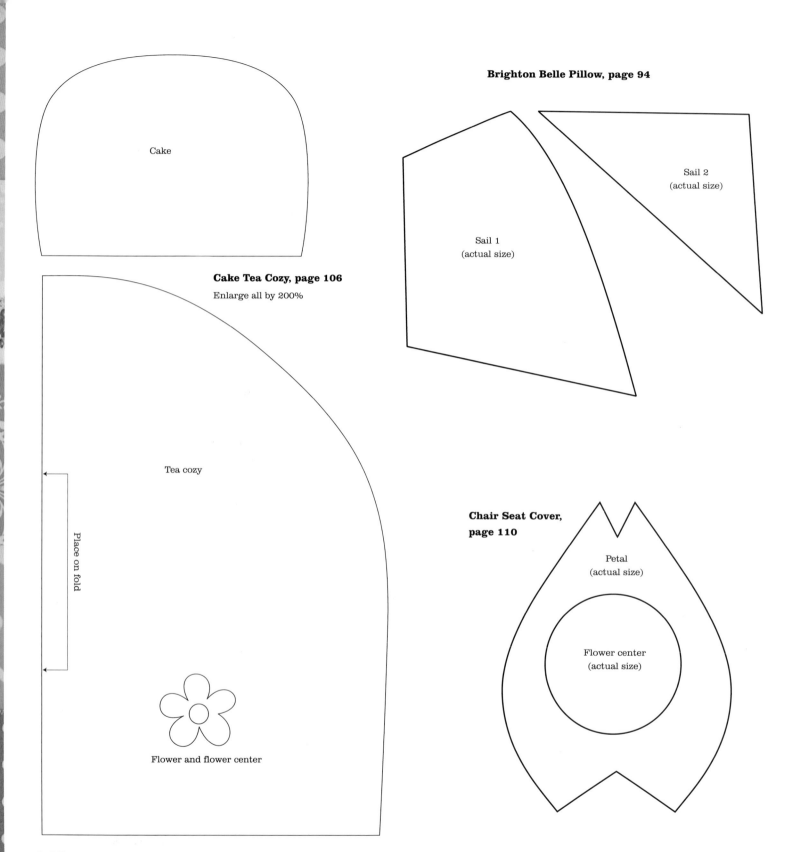

Cake

Cake Tea Cozy, page 106

Enlarge all by 200%

Tea cozy

Place on fold

Flower and flower center

Brighton Belle Pillow, page 94

Sail 1
(actual size)

Sail 2
(actual size)

**Chair Seat Cover,
page 110**

Petal
(actual size)

Flower center
(actual size)

acknowledgments

This book has been a hugely satisfying journey. I wanted to approach it from a beginner's perspective and I have had a lot of help and support from a team of enthusiastic and generous people.

I'm eternally grateful to my talented family, who always have huge involvement with my books. During the design stages I had a great help from my daughter, illustration student Camilla Perkins, whose creative flair and natural ability for color and design is a pleasure to see in action. She has taught me how to incorporate illustration into sewing and helped enormously in choosing fabrics and colors.

Thanks also to my sister, Natalie, for her creative but structured input. I remember a rainy Sunday when I felt "fabricked out;" she and my niece, Rebecca, drove through the howling weather just to help me put some color options together for a bag! Thanks, girls!

My right-hand helpers: Carolyn Meggison and Duriye Foley. What would I have done without you? Their kind support and expert sewing and quilting knowledge was a saving grace and we had a lot of fun.

Special thanks also to editor Sarah Hoggett, for being so meticulous when checking the patterns, illustrations, and techniques; I'm so grateful for your commitment and hard work. Also thanks to Kate Simunek and Michael Hill for such great illustrations.

Thanks, as ever, to Cindy Richards for having so much confidence in me and allowing me to go ahead with this book, Sally Powell for ensuring that the photos and styling did my projects proud, and Pete Jorgensen for being so encouraging and a pleasure to work with.

suppliers

A good selection of fabrics will be available from the following suppliers, although it may not be possible to match the fabrics used in the projects exactly.

US

A.C. Moore
Stores nationwide
1-888-226-6673
www.acmoore.com

FabDir
www.fabdir.com

Hobby Lobby
Stores nationwide
www.hobbylobby.com

**Joann Fabric
& Craft Stores**
Stores nationwide
1-888-739-4120
www.joann.com

Michaels
Stores nationwide
1-800-642-4235
www.michaels.com

Purl Soho
(fabrics, haberdashery)
459 Broome Street
New York
NY 10013
212 420 8796
www.purlsoho.com

Quilted Angel
(fabrics)
200 G Street
Petaluma
CA 94952
707 763 0945
www.quiltedangel.com

UK

Beyond Fabrics
(fabrics)
www.beyond-fabrics.
co.uk

**The Berwick Street
Cloth Shop**
14 Berwick Street
London W1F 0PP
www.theberwick
streetclothshop

The Button Company
(ric rac, buttons,
haberdashery)
01243 775462
www.buttoncompany.
co.uk

Creative Grids
(wadding,
templates, rulers)
01664 501724
www.creativegrids.
com

Emma's Fabric Studio
(fabrics)
www.emmasfabric
studio.co.uk

Hobby Craft
Stores nationwide
0330 026 1440
www.hobbycraft.co.uk

John Lewis
Stores nationwide
www.johnlewis.com

index